AKRASIA TO ENKRATEIA

HOW TO BE MORE SELF-DISCIPLINED AND STOP PROCRASTINATING?

DR. AMIT DAS

Made with ♥ on the Notion Press Platform
www.notionpress.com

To

All my bosses and mentors who made a difference in my professional career.

"Many people spend their lives alone, strangers to themselves, because the way to genuine contentment is concealed in plain sight. The truth is that unless you have identified your genuine calling, morality, mental toughness, and hard work will never result in inner harmony. Knowing one's aim, however, is insufficient. Your progress also demands a lot of enthusiasm. It's time to get greater insight and find the solutions that have been inside you all along."

- Dr. Amit Das, Motivational Speaker, Leadership Coach , Counsellor, and Mentor.

Contents

Foreword

"Don't put things off. Delaying a difficult chore till tomorrow only allows your mind more opportunity to construct a mountain out of a potential molehill. More time for worry to undermine your confidence. Do it right away."

We all have aspirations, ambitions, and desires. We struggle to complete the jobs on time, even if we want significant results. We put off, postpone, and delay things. You are always aware of how important it is to complete a task within a certain amount of time, but you are unable to meet the deadline. Isn't it true?

- **Does it upset you to watch your friends and coworkers succeed in life when you have been in the same spot for a long time?**
- **Do you notice a decline in productivity as the minutes pass?**
- **Do you want to objectify all of your aspirations?**

If so, you should focus on increasing your productivity. The enemies of maximum productivity; how to avoid distractions; how to form the habit of planning; and the significance of getting enough sleep.

"Procrastination is like using a credit card; it's enjoyable while it lasts, but then you have to pay the bill." -Christopher Parker

Your output, or more simply expressed, how much you can generate or provide over the course of a certain period, is referred to as your productivity. For instance, at work, productivity refers to your effectiveness and contribution to the production of the organisation. If if you are ineffective and produce little, your organisation won't gain much from you but your production is low and your productivity potentialilities are high, still your organisation won't gain much from you.

This book will provide you with incredible advice on how to increase your productivity and achieve success in all you do. See how much more productive you become by adhering to these rules. Learn how to increase productivity, create a better work environment, prioritise tasks more effectively, and improve your focus.

- **Are you sick of putting things off till the last minute, squandering time on activities you don't really love, or being unproductive?**
- **Are you prepared to stop procrastinating and start being productive, to stay alert and focused all day, and to have a feeling of success at the end of the day?**
- **Do you believe your lack of productivity is a result of your laziness?**

Your mind isn't idle; it just has to be trained with a new set of behaviors. This is something is admirable about the author. He gets more specific with each book, which helps us better grasp how we function and reduces procrastination. He hints at how we might go in the direction of success. There are jewels on every page. In order to reduce or remove the distractions that lead to delays and procrastination, the author dives into how behaviour matters and offers tactics and processes to do so. The author has offered approaches to aid in directing the reader in the proper direction, from how you live your everyday life to how successful you are in your chosen vocation.

- **Do you find it difficult to keep your commitments?**
- **Do you struggle to complete the things you start?**
- **Do you usually find an excuse?**
- **Do you struggle to break harmful habits like smoking or binge eating?**
- **Do you consistently spend more than you make each month?**

If the majority of these questions were answered in the affirmative, you most certainly lack self-discipline.

"Self-discipline is the single attribute that ensures ongoing and sustained achievement in all parts of life."

There are many key traits that contribute to a person's success, happiness, and self-actualization. Developing self-discipline is essential for accomplishing a variety of life objectives, including weight loss, increased productivity at work, and improved financial literacy.

Anyone who struggles with developing self-discipline, procrastination should read this book. All the chapters in the book on the cost of self-sabotage to be quite convincing and illuminating. Now you have constructive techniques to help your position correctly rather than shoot yourself in the foot. You will realise that avoiding important tasks is a habit that has to be broken. There is no reason to dodge the issue. The author has taken his own achievements and disappointments and turned them into some useful and doable measures for the future. If you procrastinate, as many of us do, you need something practical and actionable. According to the author, the reward is in the trip, and the adventure he will lead you on will motivate, stretch, and improve your life.

It also helps you feel more deeply connected to the meaning of life. With the help of these suggestions, you may better manage your life and find things to be simpler than before. You can achieve your short- and long-term goals by following certain recommended measures. You can avoid procrastination temptations by following the advice. This book's main goal is to increase your productivity.

On the sports field, in the boardroom, or at the dinner table, toughness has long been seen as the path to success and overcoming adversity. However, the dominant paradigm has encouraged a mindset centred on fear, fake confidence, and covering up any indication of vulnerability. In other words, we have been let down by the outdated toughness model. He shows us how to engage with our bodies, showing us that growing inner strength can truly be seen in feeling discomfort, leaning in, paying attention, and making space for deliberate action. He flips the script on what it means to be resilient. He is smart and wise all at once. He offers a road map for managing life's problems and reaching high performance that will make us happier, more successful, and, ultimately, better people by drawing from mindfulness, neuroscience, psychology, and philosophy.

This book gives precise, trustworthy advice on time management. Because the author shared his personal experiences, the information in this book is really useful and applicable to me.

We all have 24 hours each and every day to do as we like. Some people opt to have dull, uninteresting lives, while others want to advance in life and enjoy themselves.

Which kind of person do you wish to bc or identify as? He wants to give you the upper hand so you can make the most of each and every one of the limited number of hours we are granted each day. In his book, he demonstrates his thought in a humorous and straightforward manner how you can use simple hacks and techniques to boost your productivity. In addition, he'll teach you some awesome tricks that can help you save money, improve your health, and generally have more fun in life.

Few people are honest about how challenging it is to operate a business, even if many people rave about how wonderful it is to start one. He examines the issues that managers face on a daily basis, offering the knowledge he has gathered by creating, running, purchasing, selling, investing in, and managing his consulting firm.

In order to eliminate distractions and ultimately be able to work on your goals without difficulty, you must read and abide by the advice in this book. You will adore this book if you enjoy clear techniques, useful exercises, and straightforward instruction. The capacity to focus is getting harder and harder to accomplish in the world of today, when there are distractions everywhere.

We are continuously aroused and restless, sometimes without understanding why.

We suddenly discover a surplus of other things to do when it's time to go to work. We take a stroll, have a coffee, or check our emails instead of working toward our objectives. Except for the things we need to be doing, everything seems like a terrific idea.

- **Do you continually put things off?**
- **Are you fidgety and unable to concentrate on your work?**
- **Do you have a hard time getting pumped up for big goals?**
- **Do you see yourself in the scenario above?**

So, don't be alarmed. Simply put, you're overstimulated. If so, a book like this may be necessary. You will discover what procrastination truly is and when it becomes chronic in this book. Additionally, you'll learn the groups into which procrastinators fall. You'll discover certain strategies that, if you put them into practise, will help you stop procrastinating forever, as well as the warning indicators that someone is a procrastinator.

This book will teach you how to manage your time effectively so that you may profit from it no matter who you are or what you do. You'll discover when to say no without feeling horrible about yourself and how to create limits. You'll discover how to establish a productive morning routine that will significantly boost your output for the remainder of the day. You'll also discover how to prioritise your tasks, which is a key component of efficient time management, as well as other helpful information. You will also learn how to avoid distractions, stay focused, and complete more tasks in less time, as well as if multitasking is a talent that may help or hurt your time management efforts.

- **How would you like to go through any justification, difficulty, or obstruction and eventually act right away to accomplish your objectives?**
- **Are you feeling trapped, perplexed, and unsure of what to do next?**
- **Are you a stickler for detail who is always checking and worried about perfection?**

The author discussed how young professionals today have become puppets who try to engage in significant multitasking, dealing with various emails and tasks, in this book. He also discussed how professionals today have learned to value quantity over quality. As a result, they are unable to perform "deep work," which is concentrated labour free from all other outside distractions. This implies that modern professionals should get their priorities straight. He supports his ideas using concepts from psychology and neuroscience. He goes into detail on how to enhance one's cognitive talents and how companies ought to urge staff members to avoid using quick cuts to do tasks. He contends that spending some time alone to reflect and rewind while avoiding technology and social media is the best way to escape the corporate race. To produce work that is productive and effectively delivered, he upholds non-technophile principles.

You may put your life back in order with the aid of this book, which is the solution to all of your problems.

Dr. Amit Das, the author, has deepened the subjects of self-help, psychoanalysis, and performance enhancement in his research. He has developed a distillation of all of this, followed by interactive, step-by-step activities that will help you get your life back on track.

This book may be a useful resource for all who are currently having trouble and are frustrated with how excuses affect their output. When you want to produce and take action, procrastination may be a very challenging problem to deal with. You may be hampered and unable to do any tasks because of it. You owe it to yourself to discover a solution if procrastination is an issue for you. In the end, this book makes it simpler for writers to pursue their passions.

- **Have you ever had the impression that there aren't enough hours in the day to get everything done?**
- **Do your never-ending to-do lists lead you to feel pressured, nervous, and worried?**

You have, at some point in your life, encountered undesirable distractions that prevented you from concentrating on achieving your objectives. Whether you want to start your own business, teach, learn, or are a stay-at-home parent, this book will teach you how to overcome procrastination and have a fulfilling life. We all have goals, no matter how large or small, and life can get very dismal if we don't accomplish them as the days, weeks, months, and years pass by without any progress being made.

The author describes how you may use technology to both shield yourself from what is least important and serve as a reminder of what is most vital. He also gives suggestions for staying focused in this day of nonstop technology and other distractions. One thing, though, hasn't changed. He gets to the heart of what's essential for efficient time management: decision, discipline, and resolve. This game-changing book will make sure you do more of your crucial duties right now!

These objectives may seem out of reach, yet gaining money and being happy are talents we can master. So what are these abilities, and how can we learn them? Getting rich is not just about luck, and happiness is not just a trait we are born with. What are the guiding concepts that ought to direct our work? What does true progress entail? He is a life coach, thought leader, counsellor, and value investor whose ideas on accumulating riches and finding lasting happiness have enthralled people all around the world.

This book offers compelling advice about independence, setting priorities, and leading an inspired life. It exposes the keys to success. You will gradually come to understand:

- **How to avoid life's biggest traps and simply go beyond any obstacles that stand in your way?**
- **How to live a passionate life and increase your positivity?**
- **How to find your heart's desire and discover your genuine passion and purpose?**
- **How to keep your joy and discover your real calling?**

Never waste time again.By acting differently, you may start making the most of each day and achieving all of your goals. Everyone of us has the ability to regain control over our time and productivity. In the midst of our constantly connected lives, the pinging of our phones, and our increasingly hectic schedules, we've just lost sight of it. If you manage your time well, you'll do more and make more money. The key to success is focusing on and completing the most important tasks on one's to-do list.

All those points have been captured in this part of the book to show what his mentors and well-wishers feel about this book and have shared their thoughts to make it an effective piece of advice for your success.

Once again, thank you for taking the time to learn more about how you would reframe your mental attitude towards everyday situations to find a positive perspective in your life? Thank you for taking the time to read this book.

Carpe diem.

Dr. Amit Das

Leadership Coach , Counsellor, and Mentor.

Preface

"Those who have broken the bonds of procrastination, those who find joy in completing the task at hand, are the truly happy individuals. They are bursting with zeal, productivity, and desire. You have the ability to be one of them." -Norman Vincent Peale

Our most valuable resource is time, so mastering its efficient use is crucial. The majority of us are aware of this, yet balancing demanding schedules makes it all too easy to forget that there is a significant distinction between hard labour and smart work. This advice is the perfect cure for individuals who always feel like there isn't enough time in the day. You'll develop effective time management skills as a result of your extraordinarily high output. Start managing the challenging tasks that are ahead of you by cutting back on everyday distractions and keeping your attention focused.

- **Do you desire to live a life free of mess and disarray but are unsure of where to begin?**
- **Are you worn out and weighed down by things?**

You probably haven't considered how decluttering may boost your productivity, but it can. The absence of clutter makes life simpler in many aspects. To put it simply, less is more. You can work more quickly. Simply because you started by simplifying your life, you can even clean your house faster and do everything on your "to do" list faster. Getting rid of clutter is not the only aspect of decluttering. It also has psychological effects. Whether you realise it or not, your mind is always racing with ideas that are relevant to every aspect of your existence. You will discover strategies in this book that will enable you to work more effectively.

You'll have a clearer head. Simply because you find your burden manageable for the first time in a long time and don't have to worry about getting everything done, your house will be cleaner, and you could start to help people in your professional life. If you use the exercises in this book as a guide, you'll discover that life just flows more smoothly. You'll do tasks more quickly—and, more importantly, you'll complete them correctly! In order to finally stop feeling overworked and stressed, increase your productivity right now. Reduce stress and time spent working, and accomplish more!

If you're not having the life you want, maybe it's time to learn positive mind control, NLP, and manipulation through studying human behavior. If you think that manipulation is wrong, you'll discover otherwise after using our step-by-step plan to acquire what you desire. Success need not come at the expense of other people. Instead, you may enlist the aid of others, who will then share in the rewards of your accomplishment. The book vividly illustrates human behaviour in all of its complexity, exposing its weaknesses, assets, and motivations. It teaches students how to effectively employ and maximise behavioural patterns.

How to do more work in less time by avoiding distractions?

You probably fall into the category of people who put off

fulfilling their obligations until the last minute and then feel bad about it. Your responsibilities have likely been neglected and put off for so long that you have stopped seeing them, much like an outdated decoration on a bookcase. You watch cat videos on the Internet because you lack the ability to organise your priorities. But how does all of this make you feel at the end of the day when you are by yourself and overwhelmed by guilt for not even hitting one of your objectives and not even coming close to them? Stop putting off starting, take charge of your life, and give the procrastinator in you the boot!

The readers of this book are given a step-by-step process for increasing productivity and succeeding in both their personal and professional lives. In the book, important ideas are covered, including how to set reasonable goals, make a daily schedule, use tools and techniques to stay organised and on track, delegate and outsource tasks, stay focused and avoid distractions, stay motivated and stick to your time management plan, maintain a positive attitude and mindset, and dispel common myths about time management. Anyone who wants to take charge of their time, increase their productivity, and accomplish their goals should read this book. People shout out in public every day that they want to change. However, what they really desire is for everyone and everything to change except for themselves. It should go without saying that if you don't make any adjustments, nothing will change. If that's the case, why not take advantage of the possibility of living a spectacular and contented life?

How would you feel if you could avoid all distractions, even kitten videos, maintain concentration on the day's most crucial activities, accord them the appropriate priority, remove obligations and responsibilities from your to-do list, and conclude the day with contentment and a clear head?

Are you sick and tired of putting off your goals for "tomorrow"? There is no tomorrow. Am I correct? For two years, I've put off and postponed my desire to write a book. I was continually making up justifications, such as "it's not the proper moment." Alternatively, "I need to conduct additional research." But in 2015, I had had enough of the continual waiting and decided to act. My first book was released a year later, in 2016. Look, we all have a certain amount of time. And each minute brings us a little bit closer to passing away. That shouldn't frighten you. That ought to inspire you! Time is short, therefore we must act now to fulfil our desires.

I've chosen the best of my research to help you beat procrastination, increase productivity, and accomplish all you've ever desired. In addition, I went into great detail about my life and work philosophy at the beginning. This book teaches you how to understand why we procrastinate and how to stop it. Techniques for boosting productivity without becoming stressed out How to make your life more fulfilling so that you may enjoy it more. Do you feel prepared to begin reading this book? If so, act now rather than later.

- **Are you continuously delaying important things until the last minute, resulting in a chaotic life?**
- **Do you feel unorganised at both work and home?**

With all of your unfinished work, do you sometimes feel stressed, angry, or helpless? If so, it's time to overcome analysis paralysis, increase productivity, and put in place a tried-and-true method for improving self-discipline. You will discover how to stop self-talking negatively and beat procrastination to put an end to the turmoil of task avoidance. You'll learn how to break bad habits and eliminate self-sabotage in this hands-on, practical approach book, so you can stop feeling guilty about being sluggish.

This book is organised to help you save time, have more mental energy, and learn how to think with confidence. You'll discover how to focus your attention on important goals, get rid of overwhelm, and improve both your job and personal life.

Put an end to procrastination gradually. The procrastinator's mind tries to comprehend procrastinators' actions within their world without passing judgement on them. I've studied the psychology of procrastination and can provide you with techniques and solutions that have been proven to reduce procrastination and motivate people to develop discipline. Instead of merely preaching increased productivity at work, I adopt a more intimate and familiar method that impacts the reader's entire life and sense of self-respect. The book dives thoroughly into and examines subjects like self-efficacy, assertiveness, identity, fear, emotion, thinking, and the impact of these factors on procrastination. Procrastination frequently results from tasks we avoid because we are afraid of how they may affect our confidence, effort, or skill.

Do you frequently put things off for a future date that never comes? Do you prioritise less significant activities first to put off focusing on your more difficult ones? If so, immediate action is for you. Even the most successful individuals put off starting things. We all do it, but if you see that you're putting things off longer than is healthy for you, it might be time to take action. In this book more particularly, you'll discover how to identify the actual causes of your procrastination (they may not always be what you believe). Create a straightforward action plan to combat your innate procrastination tendencies, organise your thinking, and gain momentum to easily progress toward your goals. So, reduce distractions, develop laser-like focus, and many other things.

You'll receive brief workouts every day to help you better understand and combat procrastination. You'll have a straightforward yet efficient method in place by the end of the seven days to assist you in finishing your most crucial chores. So, are you prepared to stop putting off achieving your objectives and start moving forward? You will adore this book if you enjoy clear techniques, useful exercises, and straightforward instruction.

The fact is that if you delay, this terrible habit is preventing you from succeeding in a number of ways. If you don't deal with this problem, you'll have a lower chance of succeeding in your main objectives. Procrastination may result in a number of detrimental life-altering problems, such as poor academic achievement, subpar work performance, unhealthy eating habits, health problems, and financial troubles. You must thus concentrate on overcoming your procrastination tendencies by developing what is known as "the anti-procrastination habit." You'll find a wealth of knowledge to combat your procrastinating habits, regardless of whether you sometimes let tasks fall through the cracks or habitually put things off until the last minute.

There are several causes of missed deadlines, and each issue needs a unique remedy. Setting the proper expectations is the first step in coming up with the correct response. You will discover the causes of missed deadlines in this little book, along with practical advice for resolving the issue. The biggest threat to our ability to be productive is what we are. We impose our own restrictions. Start searching inside rather than outside to see why the person after you is able to do more than you and is more successful than you. There are obviously certain things you cannot control, but you must focus your attention on things you can truly control rather than obsessing over things beyond your control and being upset you are included in that. You have the secret to productivity. Everything depends on how much work you are willing to put in or how hard you are prepared to push yourself to achieve your goals. Sadly, not everything turns out as expected. We fight battles every day. We come face to face with our greatest adversaries, namely those who hinder production. It is imperative that you get to know these foes before engaging in combat with them. Recognising them is the first step in defeating them. You must research them and comprehend their origins. You can only determine the most efficient strategy for defeating them in this way.

Doing what you do best is arguably the greatest approach to providing value; we tend to place more importance on being busy than on being useful. It's critical to eliminate obstacles and sources of friction so you can concentrate on your areas of expertise and high-value work without being pressured to produce low-quality work due to time restraints. not just for financial benefits but also for your own happiness and the ability to spend more time with those that matter to you. Manage your daily chores in your notebook with this book, which includes an explanation of the "Eisenhower Matrix" and more to help you get things done or even manage your spending, and stop being reactive and only putting out fires. How far you want to go with this is up to you to decide. We all occasionally feel a little lazy, but if your lack of motivation is ongoing and you can't seem to get anything done, it's time to let go of childish mental habits, live life as an adult, and figure out your actual calling. You won't even come close to realising your potential until you choose a compelling cause. I've discussed these and other reasons for procrastination in this guide, along with some thoughtful solutions. Here is a tried-and-true manual on quitting procrastination, where you will learn:

- How to avoid letting procrastination ruin your life?
- A tried-and-true method to stop procrastinating.
- Keep your calendar organised to avoid procrastination indefinitely.
- A hot special on how to make every minute of every day count.
- Growth techniques to break your habit.

And after you have mastered this method, you won't be able to stop the revolt that will take over your life. This book is written so that you may finish it in one sitting without putting it off and allowing procrastination to rule your life once more. The issue is that starting chores when you put them off is really tough. There is no stopping once you recognise the core causes of your procrastination and what keeps you going in circles.

Your productivity must be really high if you want to ensure that you succeed in various aspects of your life and realise your aspirations. You won't be able to pursue your aspirations or accomplish your objectives if this doesn't take place. You've come to the correct site if you're wondering how to enhance your productivity and efficiency. Time is as important as your actual life, yet it's so easy to waste it on mindless Internet browsing, bad TV, or putting off tasks we know we should be doing.

A productive individual isn't busier than you are and doesn't have more time in the day than you do. The emphasis is the key distinction. A successful person can sort through the clutter and foolishness of life to focus on the important things, such as meaningful employment, satisfying relationships, self-improvement, or anything else they value.

An established method or process that establishes the right or recognised manner to carry out a task and specifies the rules that apply in a certain context is described as a "protocol" by an online dictionary. You may create protocols for the routine activities in your life as an individual, which can increase productivity and decrease delays in achieving your goals. This book offers tried-and-true guidelines for increasing productivity through a set of processes.

Making better use of the resources and abilities you currently possess is what productivity is all about, not becoming an ultra-productive superhuman.

Success need not come at the expense of other people. Instead, you may enlist the aid of others, who will then share in the rewards of your accomplishment. This book is a great overview of a changing field and a great place to start for individuals looking to further their knowledge of the mind. The book vividly illustrates human behaviour in all of its complexity, exposing its weaknesses, assets, and motivations. It teaches students how to effectively employ and maximise behavioural patterns. You will be guided through easy, realistic, and practical steps to establish a system for maximum productivity that has the potential to completely transform your life. You'll do tasks more quickly—and, more importantly, you'll complete them correctly! In order to finally stop feeling overworked and stressed, increase your productivity right now. Reduce stress and time spent working, and accomplish more!

It covers everything from setting realistic goals to cultivating a growth mindset and creating a strong support system. This book can be a priceless tool for anybody wishing to take charge of their profession and find sustainable success thanks to its simple, short writing style and countless real-world examples.

"It's time to make a change. It's time to start winning the war that has overtaken your life—the war against procrastination—instead of losing it. Stop being cruel to yourself, improve your self-control and discipline, and do whatever it takes to get rid of the tension and anguish that procrastination causes."- Dr. Amit Das

Acknowledgements

*At the outset, I will thank my family for supporting me throughout the journey of writing my book and encouraging me to live my dreams; my son has always been instrumental in giving his inspiration to complete the writing of this book. Despite the fact that I am listed as the author of this book, "**AKRASIA TO ENKRATEIA**" would not have been published if I had depended entirely on my own talents. Creating this book required more than anything—it took a family of dedicated and caring people who were always prepared to lend a hand.*

Writing a book while working full-time is no simple task, so I'd want to express my gratitude to my amazing coworkers who act as cheerleaders in equal measure. Thank you, too, to my students and clients for your patience and unflinching support while I worked on this book!

Thank you to everyone who has listened to me argue for doing everything you can to make your life, including your work life, more progressive. I appreciate everyone's assistance throughout the process. This book would not have been possible without each of you having had an impact on my life in some manner.

Lastly, I would like to thank all the people with whom I have been associated. You gave me power. I would like to thank Notion Press for publishing my book. Finally, thank you all for gifting your time to read this book.

I'd want to convey my heartfelt appreciation to the almighty God for bestowing his blessings and being so gracious.

CHAPTER ONE

Akrasia: A Nuisance or Nemesis?

"Neither a wise man nor a brave man lies down on the tracks of history to wait for the train of the future to run over him." - Dwight D. Eisenhower

Akrasia is the feeling of knowing that doing something would be beneficial for you but choosing not to do it anyhow. One of the most pervasive and persistent obstacles to action is anxiety. Akrasia is a long-standing issue, and arguments regarding its origin may be found in works by Plato, Socrates, and Aristotle. The Greek word akrasia, which means "lacking control over oneself," is the source of the word. Akrasia is a lack of self-control or procrastination. The thing preventing you from completing what you started is anxiety. The propensity of thc human brain to value present rewards more highly than future benefits is known as a behavioural inclination.

The state of acting against your better judgement is known as akrasia. It occurs when you act in a certain way even when you know you ought to act differently. Akrasia is loosely interpreted as procrastination or a lack of self-control. The thing preventing you from completing what you started is anxiety.

Aristotle contended that Akrasia results from erroneous beliefs about what someone "should" do, contrary to Plato and Socrates, who saw it as a moral flaw. "Weakness of will" is how the Stanford Encyclopedia of Philosophy describes akrasia. Akrasia has deeper stems, though. Without adding it to your to-do list, there's the sense that you "should" accomplish something.

When you are considering altering a habit you no longer desire (such as "I should stop drinking") or starting a new set of behaviours (such as "I should start processing my emails every day"), you feel anxiety. The notion that one "should" does not, however, result in action.

The topic posed by the smoker is addressed in a more broad context by Protagoras. Socrates, the representative of Plato, poses the question: Why would one behave differently if they believed a particular behaviour to be the best course of action? Since "no one moves voluntarily toward the terrible," Socrates concludes that individuals will always take the path of action they believe to be best. In other words, for Socrates, akrasia does not exist. Instead of someone purposefully acting in a way they know is wrong, misbehaviour more often results from ignorance of what exactly is right.

Accordingly, in his opinion, someone would easily quit smoking if they truly felt that they should. Socrates does concede that a person who appears to behave against their better judgement may claim that their actions are motivated by the pleasure they provide. However, he sees this as a contradiction in terms because their claim really reads as "I knew that conduct was terrible, but I was overpowered by my perception of its value."

Regarding akrasia, Aristotle disagrees with Plato. In contrast to his teacher's strictly academic approach, he adopts a strategy that is more grounded in real-world experience.

According to Aristotle, humans' recognition of akrasia is natural. He does, after all, support two separate varieties of akrasia. The first is driven by haste, or more particularly, passion, which can cause a failure in judgement and lead someone astray from what they (still) consider to be righteous deeds.

Let's momentarily deprive smokers of the spotlight and instead focus on the heroin addict as an example. Heroin gives the user a great deal of pleasure, but this does not mean that heroin addiction is healthy. Can abusing a substance that increases the risk of overdosing, choking on vomit, or dying from severe vein damage ever be justified, regardless of the pleasure it may provide? Although there may not be a clear-cut philosophical solution to this, it at least calls Socrates' and Plato's point of view into doubt.

As it describes numerous circumstances, including the heroin example, this theory looks more logical than Plato's method. The tremendous pleasure brought on by such substances can lead to a slip in judgment. Addiction or even pleasure, however, are by no means the only manifestations of this illness. Other emotions, like rage, might impair our judgement as well. Think about a contentious debate. In the excitement of the moment, people frequently say things that are obviously not entirely thought through; they may go off topic, utter petty insults, or go too far. In this case, the individual is so overcome with rage that they act without giving their actions much thought. We might say that the insult is quickly forced out of one's lips by one's ego rather than being carefully considered by one's superego. Aristotle compares these occurrences to "hurried slaves who hurry out before they have heard the full of what one says and then jumble the order" in his Nichomachean Ethics (350 BCE). The servants don't carefully consider their action before taking it; instead, they just do it.

Akrasia is one of the most prevalent and pervasive obstacles to getting things done, along with procrastination. My study suggests that having a plan of attack against Akrasia is helpful.

Aristotle flips the Socratic diagnosis of akratic ignorance. Aristotle argues that a person's ignorance leads them to be misled by pleasure, as opposed to a person being deceived by pleasure into ignorance of what is good. It may come as no surprise that Aristotle comes to the opposite conclusion, namely, that akrasia does exist. Let's bring back the smokers who are eager to stop, even if they may have hoped to avoid additional investigation. When a person makes the decision to quit smoking and finds it difficult to follow through, it is not their capacity for rational thought that is at fault. They have thought about smoking and come to the conclusion that it is unhealthy and that they should give it up, but they are unable to put this decision into action. This is what Aristotle means when he talks about willpower being weak.

Aristotle describes the second kind of akrasia as being brought on by weakness. The weak individual thinks and reasons correctly, in contrast to the passionate one. Their practical application of their well-reasoned conclusion is where they fall short.

The two categories of akrasia proposed by Aristotle remain valid today. For instance, a lot of academics have written about the disengagement of the will; however, some believe this might differ from the second sort of akrasia described by Aristotle. For instance, Richard Holton offers two somewhat different explanations for why a person who accepts the vegetarians' arguments would decide against giving up meat. The first example he presents is of a guy who constantly vows to switch to a plant-based diet only to "find himself surrendering time and again in the face of rare steaks and slow-cooked offal," as Holton so adorably puts it in "Weakness of Will and Practical Irrationality". He also provides a second example of a man who agreed with the idea of giving up meat in theory but never intended to do so in actuality. He claims that while both situations show acting against one's better judgement, only the first one demonstrates weak will. This is not to claim that there must always be these two distinct sorts; rather, it is to emphasise that just because something is akratic does not imply that it is a sign of a weak will.

The late Donald Davidson also made the case in Essays on Actions and Events (1980) that earlier philosophers were mistaken to confine akrasia to those who had come to a decision but were compelled to go in a different direction. He included any revised conclusion in the equation, such as the case of someone who typically believed it is unreasonable for them to just give in to their wants but chose to enjoy them anyhow. According to Davidson, a person's akratic behaviour in this situation is the result of their believing for a short period of time that one course of action is better than the other.

It is challenging to accept Plato's claim that acting against one's better judgement doesn't occur, regardless of which cause one thinks is most plausible. Here, it appears that Plato takes the initiative with theory rather than with experience or proof.

This is consistent with other tenets of his philosophy; after all, he does think that the physical world is an illusion. The two types of akrasia described by Aristotle appear logical, but the sort of explanation put forth by Ainslie and many other modern psychologist-influenced philosophers also seems tenable. Since there is no inevitable conflict between them, it is possible that many explanations might be accurate. For example, Ainslie's theories could serve as a third option in addition to impulsiveness and frailty. Whatever the case, it is illogical to infer from the statement that "no one walks deliberately towards the terrible" that everyone always acts against their better judgement. Any of us may look into our own lives and discover a wealth of akrasia.

"A task, a desire or wish, a "should," and an emotional sense of resistance are the four main components of akrasia."-John Koffman

Numerous contemporary psychologists have noted that the human personality is comprised of numerous, more or less distinct "sub-egos": at different times, we are a parent, a kid, a teacher, a student, an employee, a friend, an adversary, a moralist, a sensualist, etc. It is extremely important to coordinate these many elements into a unified whole rather than a disorganised mess of opposing thoughts and deeds. In this view, effective self-government is referred to as enkrateia, while its absence (a disordered, chaotic personality) or lack of self-government is referred to as akrasia.

There are several possible causes of resistance within this framework. John Koffman provides illustrations that might undoubtedly aid in determining whether you are going through Akrasia:

- What you want is impossible to define.
- You sense that the work will push you in the direction of something undesirable.
- You are unable to determine how you will go from where you are to where you want to be.
- Your idealisation of the desired outcome causes your mind to predict a low likelihood of success.
- Someone else, not you, set the "should."
- While the reward for the work at issue will arrive much later, a competing action in the present environment promises instant satisfaction.
- While other potential acts could result in more immediate and concrete advantages, this one has abstract and far-off rewards.

Akrasia is the condition in which you are aware that you ought to act but do nothing.

The idea of Akrasia is similar to the commitment to self-control and autonomy that the executive self makes to itself. It also serves as the foundation for commitments made to other individuals regarding responsibility, or rather, justifications for the sporadic failures and exceptions.

People have put things off for a long time. Even successful artists like Victor Hugo are susceptible to daily distractions. In fact, the issue is so persistent that ancient Greek philosophers like Socrates and Aristotle coined the term "akrasia" to characterise this kind of conduct.

Human behaviour is complicated, and we interpret it using a web of ideas that are in turn products of culture and philosophy. Although you might think that this proves you are a passive procrastinator, the majority of us are actually active ones. We put off our task without good reason and just because we can. Attempting to "own" the behaviour could be preferable to blaming other factors. What is will, therefore, since "akrasia" is typically defined as "weakness of will"? What is mind, therefore, if volition is some ill-defined capacity of "mind"? What is "self" if the mind is an active presence within it? and so forth.

Victor Hugo promised to write a book but put it off for more than a year? Why do we commit to objectives, set deadlines, and create plans but then fail to carry them out? Akrasia also refers to a loss of self-control in the sense of acting against reason. A person with akrasia develops the entrenched habit of allowing the non-rational aspects of their psyche to influence their reasoning faculties. Reason frequently directs action in a variety of ways. Therefore, akrasia is intriguing since it entails deviating from a standard. After reading this chapter, you will have adequate answers to the questions listed below.

- **Why we do hard things last?**
- **The cost of self-sabotage?**
- **How to minimising excuses, and the science of delaying gratification?**
- **How to automate your repeatative tasks?**

- **Identify your bottlenecks?**
- **How to adopt 80/20 principle to remove procrastination?**
- **How to control distraction and improve focus at work?**
- **How to reduce work related stress?**
- **How to program your environment with inspirational visual triggers?**
- **How to employ the premeck principle and temptation building?**
- **How to break anxiety and overwhelming?**

You may assume that something with the potential to drastically alter someone's life would necessitate attending one or more protracted seminars or perhaps enrolling in an expensive month-long program. That is undoubtedly untrue, though, as you may obtain the same advantages with this book while relaxing in your own living room.

What is Procrastination?

Procrastination was a practise that was familiar to ancient Greek philosophers. Humans have historically lacked self-control and willpower and acted contrary to our better judgement. This was known as akrasia in Greek. Its pronunciation is "ah-craze-ee-ah," which means "lack of command." Akrasia is what causes you to snooze your alarm or put things off until later in different ways.

Procrastination's etymological root is thc Latin word procrastinare, which means to postpone until later. However, it goes beyond merely postponing voluntarily. The word "procrastination" comes from the Greek word "akrasia," which means acting against our better judgement. The fact that procrastination makes us feel so bad is due, in part, to our self-awareness. When we put off completing a task, we are conscious of the fact that doing so is probably not a good idea.

Procrastination is a means of dealing with difficult feelings and unpleasant moods brought on by some jobs, including boredom, worry, insecurity, irritation, resentment, and more. It is not a special weakness in your personality or a mystifying curse on your capacity to manage time.

Procrastination may be interpreted as "the precedence of short-term mood repair above the longer-term pursuit of desired behaviours. Simply put, procrastination refers to prioritising "the immediate necessity of controlling unpleasant feelings" above completing the work.

The ideas we have regarding procrastination frequently make us feel worse and cause us to become more stressed out. The ruminative, self-blaming thoughts that many of us experience after procrastinating are known as "procrastinatory cognitions," and there is an entire body of study devoted to them. Procrastination really helps us feel temporarily relieved, which is what makes the cycle particularly vicious. Putting off a task gives relaxation in the here and now; you've been rewarded for delaying. We also know from fundamental behaviourism that when we receive a reward, we often repeat the behavior. This is the reason why procrastination frequently occurs in cycles and quickly develops into a chronic habit.

In 2012, Dr. Sirois discovered that procrastinators frequently had high levels of stress and low levels of self-compassion. This finding suggests that self-compassion acts as "a buffer against negative reactions to self-relevant events."

In reality, several studies demonstrate that self-compassion promotes drive and personal development. It not only lessens psychological pain, which we now understand to be a major contributor to procrastination, but it also actively encourages good emotions like optimism, wisdom, curiosity, and personal initiative. The best part is that practising self-compassion doesn't call for anything outside of yourself; all it takes is a determination to face your struggles with more acceptance and kindness rather than with remorse and brooding.

Procrastination is highly existential, though, since it calls into question our autonomy as individuals and the difference between how we wish to spend our time and how we really do. But it also serves as a reminder of how similar we all are; most of us just want to be content with the decisions we make.

Nearly all heavy smokers are fully aware of the effects their tobacco habits are going to have. Even many people admit that it would be great to break the habit. Nevertheless, a significant number of these individuals smoke despite their better judgment. They could think to themselves, "Why do I keep smoking when I know it would be better not to?" in between breaths of nicotine and remorse. Smoking is an addictive activity, which is one answer to this issue but not one in common parlance.

Procrastination is the deliberate act of delaying or postponing something even when one is aware that doing so would have negative effects. Thc word is dcrived from the Latin word procrastinatus, which came from the prefix pro-, which means "forward," and crastinus, which means "of tomorrow." It is a very common human behavior. It is a typical human experience to procrastinate on mundane activities or even important ones like going to an appointment, turning in a report for work or school, or talking to a partner about a difficult subject. It can be thought of as a wise response to some demands that could present risky or negative outcomes or require waiting for new information to arrive, despite the fact that it is typically perceived as a negative trait due to its impeding effect on one's productivity and is frequently associated with depression, low self-esteem, guilt, and inadequacy.

Chronic procrastination has measurable detrimental effects on our mental and physical health over time, including chronic stress, general psychological distress, low life satisfaction, symptoms of anxiety and depression, poor health behaviours, chronic illness, chronic pain, hypertension, and even cardiovascular disease. But I thought delaying our actions would make us feel better. It's paradoxical, if that makes sense, that we delay things to put off unpleasant sensations yet end up feeling worse. Again, we owe evolution our gratitude.

It's also critical to take into account how procrastination may be impacted by various cultural ideas on time management. For instance, people tend to place a larger priority on finishing a task correctly before starting in cultures with a multi-active view of time. People in societies where time is seen linearly often set aside a specific amount of time for a work and cease after that time has passed. Students from Western and Non-Western cultures are observed to display academic procrastination, but for different reasons, from a cultural and social standpoint. While students from Non-Western cultures postpone to avoid seeming incompetent or exhibiting a lack of competence in front of their classmates, students from Western cultures prefer to procrastinate to avoid performing worse than they have in the past or failing to study as much as they should have.

According to Dr. Hershfield's research, we experience our "future selves" as strangers rather than as aspects of ourselves on a brain level. Parts of our brains genuinely believe that the chores we are delaying, as well as the unpleasant emotions that will be waiting for us on the other side, are someone else's responsibility when we procrastinate. To make matters worse, while under stress, we are even less capable of making deliberate, long-term judgments. The amygdala, often known as the "threat detector" region of the brain, sees tasks that make us feel uncomfortable or uneasy as real threats to our self-worth or general well-being. Even though we rationally understand that delaying the work would make us more stressed in the future, our brains are still wired to be more concerned with removing the threat in the here and now. This phenomenon is known as an "amygdala hijack." Sadly, we can't just tell ourselves to stop putting things off. Despite the popularity of "productivity hacks," concentrating on the issue of how to complete more work misses the mark by failing to address the underlying issue of procrastination.

"People procrastinate because they are afraid of the success that they know will result if they move ahead now. Because success is heavy, carries a responsibility with it, it is much easier to procrastinate and live on the 'someday I'll philosophy'."- Denis Waitley

According to research on the delayed-gratification behaviours of pigeons, procrastination is not just a human trait. It may also be seen in certain other species. Pigeons are known to "procrastinate," as demonstrated by studies that reveal they prefer to pick a difficult but delayed activity over a simple but urgent one.

A survey conducted in 2004 found that 70% of college students identified as procrastinators, but a study conducted in 1984 found that 50% of students would constantly postpone and regarded it as a big problem in their lives. According to research done on university students, procrastination was shown to be more common with activities that were seen as unpleasant or as burdens than with tasks for which the student thought they lacked the necessary abilities for completion.

We must understand that procrastination is really about emotions, not production. The solution does not include purchasing time management software or learning new self-control techniques. It has to do with finding new ways to control our emotions.

Our brains constantly seek out relative rewards. Our brain will just keep engaging in procrastination until we provide it with something if we have a habit loop around it and haven't found a better reward.

"Amateurs sit and wait for inspiration, the rest of us just get up and go to work."- Stephen King

We know that the act of delaying or postponing a task or group of duties is known as procrastination. It is the force that keeps you from completing the tasks you set out to perform, whether you call it procrastination, akrasia, or something else. Victor Hugo was up against an insurmountable deadline in the summer of 1830. The French novelist had promised his publisher a new book a year ago. However, he didn't write throughout that year;

instead, he pursued other endeavours, had visitors, and put off his work. Hugo's publisher expressed his frustration by establishing a deadline that would expire in less than six months. The deadline for finishing the work was February 1831.

Why did Victor Hugo promise to write a book but put it off for more than a year? Why do we commit to objectives, set deadlines, and create plans but then fail to carry them out? The propensity of the human brain to value present benefits more highly than future ones is known as "time inconsistency."

You are essentially establishing plans for your future self when you set goals for yourself, such as deciding to publish a book, lose weight, or learn a new language. When you think about the future, it is easy for your brain to see the value in making choices that will have long-term advantages. This is because you are imagining how you want your life to be in the future.

Additionally, studies have shown that the current self prefers short-term rewards over long-term gains. This is one of the reasons you might feel inspired to alter your life before bed, but when you wake up, you find yourself reverting to old habits. When they are in the future, your brain favours long-term advantages; but, when they are in the present, it prefers instant satisfaction.

"Don't put off until tomorrow what you can do today."- Benjamin Franklin

Victor Hugo was inventing a "commitment mechanism" when he kept his clothing away so he could concentrate on writing. A commitment device is a decision you make today that guides your future behavior. It is a technique for securing future behaviour, keeping you restricted from negative habits and bound to positive ones.

A commitment device can be created in a variety of ways. By buying food in individual packages rather than in bulk, you can reduce overeating. This is one of the main reasons why the capacity for delayed gratification is such an excellent indicator of life success. You may go from where you are to where you want to be by learning how to, at least occasionally, if not always, resist the want for quick satisfaction.

However, you are no longer making a decision for your future self when the time comes to make one. You are currently in the present, and your mind is considering your current state.

The behavioural economics concept of "temporal inconsistency" may help to explain why anxiety dominates our lives and procrastination draws us in.

To avoid further gambling binges, you can voluntarily request to be included on the forbidden list at casinos and online poker rooms. Even athletes who must "make weight" for a competition have been reported to leave their wallets at home the week before they weigh in in order to avoid the temptation to eat fast food.

Even if the circumstances are different, the message remains the same: commitment devices can aid in the planning of your future behavior. Instead of depending on willpower in the heat of the moment, look for ways to automate your behaviour in advance. Instead of becoming a victim of your future choices, take control of them.

So why do we still put things off? because beginning the task is difficult, not actually doing the work. The difficulty that keeps us from acting generally revolves around beginning the habit. Work is frequently less uncomfortable to perform once you have started. Due to this, it is frequently more crucial to develop the habit of starting something new than it is to worry about whether or not the new activity will be effective. You need to gradually scale back your behaviour. Build a ritual with all of your heart and soul, and make it as simple as you can to begin. Wait until you've perfected the skill of showing up before you worry about the outcomes.

Jim Rohn once said, "We must all suffer from one of two pains: the pain of discipline or the pain of regret.The difference is discipline weighs ounces while regret weighs tons."

The present self cannot be motivated by future repercussions and benefits. Instead, you need to figure out how to bring incentives and penalties from the future into the present. You need to transform the potential repercussions into actual ones.

The Relationship Between Procrastination and Action

This is precisely what takes place when we decide to stop procrastinating and start doing. Let's imagine, for illustration's sake, that you need to create a report. You've been putting it off every day for weeks despite knowing about it. You feel a tiny bit of nagging discomfort and worry as you consider the essay you have to write, but not enough to take any action. Then, all of a sudden, the future repercussions become the present repercussions the day before the deadline, and you create that report hours before it is due. When you eventually reached the "action line," the anguish of procrastination had worsened.

It's crucial to take note of this. The discomfort starts to go away as soon as you pass the action line. In reality, procrastinating is frequently more unpleasant than performing the activity in the present moment. Usually, the guilt, humiliation, and worry you experience when you put off doing anything are greater than the effort and energy you must expend when working. Not performing the task is not the issue; beginning the work is.

Making it as simple as possible for the present self to start anything and having faith that drive and momentum will follow once we start are both necessary if we wish to avoid delaying. (Motivation frequently arrives after the beginning, not beforehand.)

Why Do We Put It Off?

We have all struggled with procrastination at some point or another. We have struggled with postponing, evading, and procrastinating on important matters for as long as humans have existed.

When we momentarily learn how to quit procrastinating during our more productive periods, we feel content and successful. Today, we'll discuss how to make those infrequently occurring productive moments more common. This guide's objectives are to explain the science behind why we delay, give tried-and-true frameworks for doing so, and discuss practical tactics that will make it simpler to take action.

Okay, definitions are nice, but why do we put things off? What is happening in the brain that makes us avoid actions we know we ought to take? We should now introduce some science to our conversation. Time inconsistency is a phenomenon discovered by a behavioural psychology study that helps to explain why procrastination tends to draw us in despite our best efforts. The propensity of the human brain to value present benefits more highly than future ones is known as "time inconsistency."

Imagine that you have two selves: your present self and your future self. This will help you grasp this better. Setting objectives for oneself, such as shedding pounds, penning a book, or learning a new language, is really making preparations for your future self. You are imagining what you want the future of your life to look like. Researchers have discovered that it is quite simple for your brain to perceive the worth of making choices that will have long-term advantages when you think about your future self. In the long run, the future self prioritises benefits.

The present self is the only one who can actually carry out goals; the future self can only formulate them. You are no longer choosing for your future self when the time comes to make a decision. You are currently in the present, and your present-moment thoughts are focused on your present self. Researchers have shown that the present self prefers short-term rewards over long-term gains.

As a result, the present self and the future self frequently clash. The present self wants a doughnut, while the future self wants to be slim and fit. Yes, everyone is aware that eating well now will prevent getting overweight in ten years. However, effects like a rise in diabetes or heart failure risk won't be seen for several years.

"If you are not willing to risk the unusual, you will have to settle for the ordinary."- Jim Rohn

In a similar vein, many young people are aware of the need to save for retirement in their 20s and 30s, but many are unaware of the long-term rewards. The present self finds it far simpler to perceive the value in purchasing a new pair of shoes than it does in setting aside a huge cost for a 70-year-old you. (If you're wondering, our brain rates short-term rewards more highly than long-term benefits for a number of very valid evolutionary reasons.)

This is one of the reasons you might feel inspired to alter your life before bed, but when you wake up, you find yourself reverting to old habits. Your brain loves instant pleasure when it comes to the now, but it values long-term rewards when they are in the future (tomorrow) (today).

On the left side of your desk, there was a stack of important business documents. Your phone is on your right. Which one do you grab first? The majority of individuals would probably reach for their phones, justifying their choice with lame justifications like, "Work'll just be 5 minutes, and then I'll get right back to it," or "I just need to check my messages very quickly." Is it truly necessary? Or do you simply wish to? There is a distinction there, and you must ascertain what it is.

You may be asking yourself, "So what?" Yes, I put things off. I don't think less of myself for doing that. Of course not, but it's also not like putting off crucial responsibilities until later would benefit you in any way. Depending on where you are in life, you are also jeopardising your profession or schooling in addition to ruining the chance to have more free time. Additionally, you're endangering your general wellbeing because procrastination is a risk factor for stress, poor self-esteem, and feelings of worthlessness.

Break the procrastination habit, acccelerate your productivity, and take control of your life.

Find out how to change your behaviours and put an end to your ongoing misery. A strong strategy that will push you to finish the work at hand in only 2 minutes. The formula for striking the ideal balance between drive and restraint and creating the conditions for future success. Why procrastination isn't just another word for laziness, and how to identify the root causes of your destructive behaviours so you can break them forever.

The top causes of your procrastination habit and strategies for overcoming them. How to successfully resist temptations while still achieving the best of both worlds the risk that your routine poses to your quest to make great life changes, as well as techniques to make the process simpler for yourself.

How to get out of that risky mindset—the most important thing most people do that immediately sets you up for failure—and much more. Everyone can change their behaviors, no matter what stage of life they are in or whether they have always thought of themselves as chronic procrastinators.

Nothing worthwhile happens without a lot of patience and work, even if the change may demand both.

You may improve your emotional and mental health as well as your chances of getting promotions, career advancements, or better grades by using the appropriate procrastination-busting methods. Stop wasting any more of your valuable time and start making the necessary changes to get everything in order. No more waiting! Every second you waste idly scrolling around social media rather than getting things done is time that is wasted.

The Biggest Reasons For Procrastination

"Procrastination is the tendency to carry out less urgent activities in preference to more important ones." "It is the avoidance of accomplishing a task that has to be performed." It is a sort of self-sabotage that can prevent someone from ever accomplishing their objectives or fulfilling their lifelong dreams.

Procrastination has been dubbed "the thief of time," "the assassin of opportunities," and "a lot of fun until you get the bill" when contrasted to using a credit card. If you want to succeed and achieve success, you must learn to control your procrastination rather than allowing it to control you. It is possible to unlearn the habit of procrastination. It is an attitude that may be changed, as well as a frame of mind.

Everyone has goals and dreams that they want to realise. The majority of individuals, in reality, never fulfil their potential or realise their goals. They are unwittingly clinging to a disempowering narrative about their capacity to fulfil their life goals. They don't think they have the capacity to do more in life, nor do they think they deserve it. A procrastinator's bad emotions draw low vibrational energy, which leads to lost time and missed chances.

We go on a binge during this period to identify and address our procrastination. By increasing awareness of the subconscious and cognitive processes within a procrastinator, this book aims to help readers procrastinate less.

- Are you a perfectionist?
- Are you fear the unknown?
- Do you promise to do it later?
- Do you focus more on finsihing east tasks first?
- Do you often experience a lack of motivation?
- Do you often get distracted?
- Are you confused how to get start?
- Are you not having control on scheduling tasks in hand?

Connection Between Your Brain And Procrastination

We just don't have enough time to do everything on our to-do list. There will never be. People who are successful don't strive to accomplish everything. They develop the ability to concentrate on and complete the most crucial activities. Their frogs are consumed. According to an old proverb, if you consume a live frog first thing each morning, you will feel relieved knowing that you have completed the toughest task of the day.

Brian Tracy compares taking on your most difficult endeavour to eating a frog; it's also the one that has the potential to make the biggest difference in your life. He teaches you how to plan your days so you can focus on these important chores and carry them out successfully.

"The adversary exists." A sophisticated, aggressive, and malicious force is working against us. Undcrstanding this is the first step. The power of this acknowledgement alone is immense. Both my life and yours will be preserved by it.

- Could you be impeding your ability to do outstanding work?

- Have you ever begun something but never finished it?
- Do you want to do important work but are unsure where to begin?

Here I will demonstrate that the solution lies not in having better ideas but in actually putting those ideas into practice. Do the work is a tool that will assist you in taking action and effectively completing tasks. It is a weapon against the resistance. Along the journey, you will point out the likely resistance points, and that will guide you through. You are not insane. You are not alone, though.

You Are In Your Comfort Zone

First, choose a peaceful spot to sit. Now close your eyes and picture the life you want to live in 10 years. Do not be concerned; this is not a wishful exercise to bring your fantasies to pass. Instead, I'm putting your deepest, most personal aspirations into words as the first actionable step. The challenging effort needed to reach your goals will follow.

When you're in your comfort zone, you're at ease in a setting you know well, which reduces your prospects for advancement.

Have we not all been there? However, the length of time spent there is what separates the successful from the average. Long-term comfort zone living leads to complacency and a failure to pursue your most important goals.

What are some objectives you've tried to achieve but haven't been able to? Have you begun healthy habits like exercising and eating well only to abandon them quickly? Or have you continuously put off completing a crucial task that you ought to have accomplished long ago?

Your comfort zone has that effect on you.

This chapter provides examples to clarify what the comfort zone is, as well as information on its risks and ways to leave it. The legendary leadership and elite performance expert Robin Sharma first introduced 5 AM club concept more than 20 years ago. It is based on a ground-breaking morning routine that has assisted his clients in maximising productivity, activating their best health, and fortifying their serenity in this era of overwhelming complexity. A famous blogger cuts through the crap in this generation-defining self-help book to teach us how to quit striving to be "positive" all the time so that we may actually improve and be happier.

How do the world's greatest minds, business moguls, and smartest individuals begin their days in order to accomplish amazing feats? Is there a little-known method you can apply right away to wake up early with a spark of inspiration, laser-like focus, and a burning desire to make the most of every day? A step-by-step plan to safeguard the peaceful early morning hours so you have time for exercise, self-care, and personal development? A neuroscience-based technique that has been shown to make it simple to get up while most others are still asleep, allowing you valuable time to yourself to think, express your creativity, and start the day pleasantly rather than hurriedly? Insider-only? strategies for shielding your dreams, abilities, and gifts from digital distractions and pointless diversions, allowing you to achieve success, influence, and a spectacular impact on the world.

"As human beings, our greatness lies not so much in being able to remake the world- this is the myth of the atomic age- as in being able to remake ourselves" – Mahatma Gandhi.

I recently finished Josh Kaufman's excellent book, "The Personal MBA." Reading this novel now makes me feel a little behind the times. I could have read it before enrolling in college and would have ended up deciding on a more suitable field of study. Nevermind. The timing is really good because I was particularly interested in the chapters on Akrasia and monoidealism. For the sake of the average reader, we may remark that procrastination and akrasia are connected but not the same.

How To Overcome Akrasia?

Procrastination frequently happens when you have made up your mind to finish a task but keep pushing it off till a later time without actively opting to accomplish it then. Procrastination, for instance, is when you have "write 200 words of introduction by 14:00" on your to-do list but spend hours on Netflix without producing a single word.

Procrastination, on the other hand, is when you know you should do something and set out the steps in a to-do list but keep putting it off because you have other, less "essential" things to accomplish, like housework.

I've been a procrastinator in the past and have also had Akrasia. You only need to start writing your thoughts and the measures to complete them to deal with the anxiety. It's essential to "bleed out" what you need to do. Get a to-do app or a notebook and jot down everything you feel like you "should" be doing.

After learning the steps, you'll need to overcome your procrastination. I've discovered that employing some of the Personal Kanban task management concepts, such as working on one item at a time until it is marked as complete and the Getting Things Done method, is the greatest way to combat procrastination. According to the task's nature and the amount of time required to finish it, the GTD principles teach you the kinds of actions you should take. Simply doing it is my recommendation. This is the proper attitude. Have self-control (enkrateia, the opposite of akrasia). Plan your future course of action and choose enkrateia over akrasia as your way of life.

The adjective enkratês is the source of enkrateia. In this context, it alludes to personal dominance or restraint. To embrace efficiency, create new habits for long-term productivity that will help you reach your goals. Breaking new behaviours down into their component components and concentrating on just getting started are two ways to start. Until you've perfected the art of showing up, don't worry too much about the outcomes. For instance, you want to read a chapter every day. But you're busy and unsure of when you'll have time to read the entire chapter.

Consider adjusting your aim as an alternative to giving up. Set a goal to read for 15 minutes if you can find the time. Set a goal to read for an hour if you can find the time. You complete your reading in this manner. Any advancement is development, no matter how slight. If your objective is to create a report and the size of the task overwhelms you, break it down into smaller steps. Working on a smaller and simpler task will make it seem more accessible and attainable, and you'll be less tempted to put it off.

Consider using commitment gadgets to create your ideal future. A commitment device is a tactic you employ to manage your behaviour so that it supports your long-term objectives. It's a strategy for limiting your options and directing yourself in the direction of your goals. Everyone engages in this, whether in their personal or professional lives, to some extent. You might only watch your favourite TV programme when doing chores like folding clothes or working out. Or perhaps you reward yourself with a coffee once the important report is finished. By giving yourself tiny prizes for achieving each step on the way to your goal, you can keep your momentum going. You'll have a better chance of completing your bigger assignments and beating Akrasis if you do this.

Victor Hugo was up against an insurmountable deadline in the summer of 1830. The French novelist had promised his publisher a new book a year ago. However, he didn't write throughout that year; instead, he pursued other endeavours, had visitors, and put off his work. Hugo's publisher expressed his frustration by establishing a deadline that would expire in less than six months. The deadline for finishing the work was February 1831. Hugo devised a bizarre strategy to overcome his procrastination.

He gathered all of his clothing and requested a helper to store them securely in a big chest. All that was left for him to wear was a big scarf. During the fall and winter of 1830, he stayed in his study and wrote frantically since he lacked the proper attire to go outside. On January 14, 1831, The Hunchback of Notre Dame was released two weeks early.

Typically, procrastination is a "yes" or "no" decision. Consider more common examples like compulsive or addictive behaviour patterns like excessive spending, manic media use, or even instigating a fight that you "know" you'll regret and that will cause you difficulty or misery.

An explanation looks beneficial since it makes a recommendation for an action based on that understanding, but occasionally, it just isn't successful. An explanation looks beneficial since it makes a recommendation for an action based on that understanding, but occasionally, it just isn't successful. Despite the fact that the concepts being described are only accepted in a completely uncritical manner, we nonetheless experience a hypnotic draw toward explanations.

Before the words leave our mouths, our brain often answers yes or no while we are deciding whether to do something or not. Prior to considering any potential benefits for other people, we first assess whatever benefits it already has. Before deciding what to undertake, we take into account additional factors, including the required time, strength, and effort. Before we commit, all of this happens in a brief second, and the response is spoken.

Procrastination frequently happens when you have made the decision to do a task but keep pushing it off without consciously opting to do it later. Procrastination is not always a negative thing. Procrastinators can be either aggressive or passive.

This picture doesn't have any alternative text. The idea of Akrasia is similar to the commitment to self-control and autonomy that the executive self makes to itself. It also serves as the foundation for commitments made to other individuals regarding responsibility, or rather, justifications for the sporadic failures and exceptions.

One reason why procrastination ensnares us and apathy governs our lives has to do with a concept from behavioural economics called temporal inconsistency. The propensity of the human brain to value present benefits more highly than future ones is known as "time inconsistency."

We are essentially establishing plans for our future selves when we set goals for ourselves, such as deciding to publish a book, lose weight, or learn a new language. When we think about the future, it is easy for our brains to see the value in doing activities that will have long-term advantages. We are imagining how we want our lives to be in the future.

But when the time comes to choose, we are no longer choosing for our future selves. Our minds are currently focused on our immediate surroundings and our present selves. Additionally, studies have shown that the current self prefers short-term rewards over long-term gains. This is one of the reasons we might feel inspired to alter our lives before going to sleep, but when we wake up, we discover that we are returning to our old habits. When they are in the future, our brain favours long-term advantages; nevertheless, when they are in the present, it prefers instant satisfaction. This is one of the main reasons why the capacity for delayed gratification is such an excellent indicator of life success. You may go from where you are to where you want to be by learning how to, at least occasionally, if not always, resist the want for quick satisfaction.

Our brains favour short-term rewards above long-term gains. It is only a result of how our thoughts function. Because of this propensity, we frequently turn to strange methods to complete tasks, like the one Victor Hugo used to lock up all of his clothes in order to write a novel. However, if our goals are significant to us, it may sometimes be worthwhile to invest effort in creating these commitment tools. As the antonym of Akrasia, Aristotle created the name Enkrateia. Akrasia describes our propensity to procrastinate, whereas Enkrateia implies to be "in control of oneself." Simple activities you may do to make it simpler to live an Enkrateia-inspired life as opposed to an Akrasia-inspired one include planning your future actions, lowering the difficulty of commencing beneficial habits, and employing implementation goals.

Plan out your future course of action. Victor Hugo was inventing a "commitment mechanism" when he kept his clothing away so he could concentrate on writing. A commitment device is a decision we make now that guides our future behavior. It serves as a mechanism to anchor future behaviour, tether us to virtuous routines, and barricade us against vices.

Even though the circumstances are different, the message remains the same: commitment devices can aid in the planning of our future deeds. Finding methods to pre-automate our behaviour rather than depending on willpower in the heat of the moment is the objective. Reduce the initial friction as a second strategy.

Usually, the agony of putting off performing the task is worse than the guilt and irritation of delaying. According to Eliezer Yudkowsky, being in the middle of performing the task is typically less painful than being in the middle of delaying.

So why do we still put things off? Because beginning the job is the difficult part, not actually doing the task. Usually, the resistance that keeps us from behaving is focused on actually beginning the activity. The task is frequently less painful to do once we have started. Because of this, it is frequently more crucial to develop the habit of starting something new than it is to worry about whether or not the new activity will be effective.

The scope of our habits has to be continually constrained. We must devote all of our time and effort to creating a ritual and making it as simple as possible to begin. We don't need to worry about the outcomes until we have perfected the art of showing up.

Law Of Procrastination

Delaying tasks causes them to take longer to complete and makes someone else responsible for their termination (i.e., the authority who imposed the deadline).

You may be familiar with the cautious but gloomy adage, "If anything can go wrong, it will," which may be applied to any situation. We call it Murphy's law. Every aspect of human existence may benefit from it, and project management is no exception. But given Murphy's rule, is there any possibility you can prevent your efforts from failing? Let's look for the solution to this query. Let's first consider the potential pitfalls after the project has been launched.

According to Wellingtone's The State of Project Management 2020, 71% of businesses are unable to complete projects on schedule, 57% are unable to do so within the allocated budget, and 60% fail to reap the full advantages of their investments. Both poor management and unfortunate circumstances brought on by Murphy's law are to blame for it.

Procrastination may take many different forms. They perform anything else in place of that one crucial activity. Some people replace it with another activity on their to-do list, one that may not be as necessary. Others go to different enjoyable pursuits, such as watching TV.

As for me, I daydream. The procedure is as follows: I sit down to begin a task, or I get up (whatever), and I begin to mentally map out the steps I'll take to finish the activity, noting any areas where I'll probably struggle. Then, even though I haven't started the work yet, I begin to consider when I'll accomplish it and how I'll reward myself. I daydream while others conduct enjoyable activities or less significant jobs to pass the time. As I mentioned before, I've read several books and watched a lot of films on the subject of procrastination, and both provide helpful tips on how to break the habit.

How To Immediately Stop Postponing Tasks?

There are several methods we may use to stop putting things off. Following an outline and explanation of each principle, I'll give you a few instances of strategy in action.

Strategy I:

Make the benefits of taking action more immediate. Procrastination may be avoided if you can discover a means to make the advantages of long-term decisions more apparent right away. The temptation bundling strategy is one of the most effective ways to make future benefits available right away. A behavioural economist at the University of Pennsylvania named Katy Milkman developed the idea of temptation bundling. Simply put, the approach advises combining a habit that is beneficial to you in the long term with one that makes you feel good right now. Listed here are a few prevalent instances of temptation bundling:

- Only indulge in your favourite podcasts or audiobooks when working out.

- Only get a pedicure while going through overdue emails for work.
- Only watch your preferred programme while doing laundry or other housework.
- If you must have your monthly meeting with a challenging coworker, only dine at your preferred restaurant.
- The basic structure is to only do [things you love] while doing [things you procrastinate on].

People put things off because they are terrified of the success that will come from starting now.

Strategy II:

Make the repercussions of delaying more immediate. You can be made to pay the price of procrastination in many different ways, and sooner rather than later. For instance, skipping your workout the next week won't have much of an effect on your life if you exercise alone. You won't see an instant decline in health as a result of skipping that one workout. Only after weeks or months of being inactive does exercising become painfully expensive. The price of skipping your workout, though, increases if you agree to work out with a friend at 7 a.m. on Monday. If you skip this workout, you'll look like a jerk. Using a service like Stickk to place a wager is another popular tactic. The money goes to a charity you despise if you don't follow through on what you claim you'll do. Putting some skin in the game and creating a new consequence that occurs if you don't engage in the activity immediately are the goals here.

The only thing that separates dreamers from those who achieve great things is following through.

Strategy III:

Plan your future course of action. A "commitment device" is one of psychologists' go-to methods for overcoming procrastination. Using commitment tools, you may quit procrastinating by planning out your future actions in advance. For instance, buying food in individual containers rather than in bulk can help you control your eating patterns in the future.

Procrastination and the "someday I'll" way of thinking are easier to practise since achievement is difficult and comes with responsibilities.

Strategy IV:

Improve the task's viability. As we've already discussed, procrastination is typically brought on by resistance to beginning an activity. Once you have started, continuing to work is frequently less unpleasant. One excellent reason to make your routines smaller is that you'll be less inclined to put things off if they're simple and quick to start. The 2-Minute Rule, which claims that "when you start a new habit, it should take less than two minutes to complete," is one of my favourite strategies for making habits simpler. The goal is to make starting as simple as possible, and once you get going, believe that momentum will drive you farther into the process.

It is easier to continue doing something once you have begun. Procrastination and laziness are defeated by the 2-Minute Rule by making it impossible to resist starting to do anything. Breaking down projects is an excellent method to make them more manageable. Take the prolific output of renowned author Anthony Trollope as an example. In addition to articles and letters, he also authored 18 nonfiction books, 12 short tales, 2 plays, and 47 novels. What was his secret? Trollope measured his progress in 15-minute increments rather than by the completion of chapters or novels. In order to achieve his goal of writing 250 words every 15 minutes, he set aside three hours each day to write in this manner.

It's crucial to make your responsibilities more manageable for two reasons. Long-term momentum is maintained by taking little steps, which increases your likelihood of completing challenging activities. Your day will take on a more proactive and effective attitude the faster you finish productive tasks.

This second criterion, which refers to how quickly you finish your first activity of the day, is very crucial for avoiding procrastination and consistently producing high-quality work. This method allowed him to continue working on the challenging task of producing a book while experiencing feelings of fulfilment and achievement every 15 minutes. By removing social networking or gaming applications from your phone, you may avoid wasting time on them. (Alternatively, you might block them on your computer.)

Similar to this, by putting your TV in a closet and only pulling it out on big game days, you may lessen the probability of mindless channel surfing. To stop future gambling binges, you can voluntarily request to be included on the forbidden list at casinos and online gaming platforms. By setting up an automated transfer of money to your savings account, you may accumulate an emergency fund. These are all illustrations of procrastination-reducing commitment gadgets.

Okay, we've discussed a range of tactics for overcoming procrastination every day. Let's now talk about some techniques for developing productivity as a lifelong habit and keeping procrastination from returning.

We don't have a clear structure in place for determining what is essential and what we should work on first, which is one reason why it is so easy to fall back into procrastination again. (This is just another illustration of how the system frequently takes precedence over the objective.) One of the most straightforward productivity strategies I've ever seen is also one of the greatest.

Using visual signals to activate your behaviours and track your progress is another approach to escaping the trap of chronic procrastination. A visual cue is something you can see that motivates you to act (a visual reminder). The reasons they are crucial for overcoming procrastination are as follows:

Visual signals serve as a reminder to begin a habit. We frequently tell ourselves lies about our capacity to establish new habits. "I'm starting to eat healthier." truly this time.But a few days later, the drive wanes and life's hustle starts to take over once more. A new habit should never be relied upon to be remembered to be done. A visual stimulus can be quite helpful in this situation.

When your surroundings push you in the correct direction, it is much simpler to maintain healthy behaviours. Visual clues show how well you are doing with a behavior. Although everyone is aware that success depends on consistency, relatively few individuals truly assess their level of consistency in daily life. Because it is a built-in measurement system, having a visible cue—like a calendar that records your progress—avoids that problem. You can gauge your progress with just a quick glance at your calendar.

The endowed progress effect is a term used in a number of well-known behavioural economics studies to describe this phenomenon. Viewing your prior achievements is a terrific technique to inspire your subsequent fruitful activity. The paper clip strategy, which is useful for overcoming procrastination day after day, and the Seinfeld strategy, which is wonderful for keeping consistency over longer periods of time, are two of my favourite visual cue-based tactics.

I sincerely hope that my quick tutorial on procrastination was helpful. Check out my whole collection of thought in this book if you're seeking additional tips on how to stop waiting and start acting. On motivation, visual signals may have a supplementary impact. It is normal to feel more driven to keep up the habit as the physical proof of your progress grows. You'll be more driven to complete the work if you can see more visible progress.

Getting Things Done Method To Stop Procrastination

In our world, there are two sorts of people: those who want to do their task as soon as possible and those who want to put it off as long as they can. This is divided into two categories: "precrastinators" in the first and "procrastinators" in the second.

Procrastination has been extensively studied and published; the majority of these studies label it as being bad for one's health and increasing stress levels. However, some "procrastinating apologists," as you may call them, say that there are certain advantages to it as well. But according to studies, procrastination has significantly more negative effects than positive ones in the short run.

Procrastination is said to be caused by a lack of discipline, according to a popular notion. Procrastinators prefer entertainment and amusement over hard labor. They don't have effective processes and practises, to use a more contemporary version of this justification. Numerous studies have demonstrated that healthy practises lessen the need for self-control. They make it simpler to maintain challenging behaviours and withstand interruptions. However, developing a habit that offers these advantages often takes a few months. Plan your serious work consistently. Focusing on your most significant long-term endeavour is how I would characterise profound work. For example, it can require creating a business plan, doing intricate data analysis, or authoring a book. Deep work is normally difficult, but if you persistently perform it every day in a regular routine, it will get easier.

Even the most successful individuals delay gratification. Procrastination may become a problem when it takes on a life of its own. Chronic procrastination is a sort of self-sabotage that can have disastrous results and lead to an unhappy and painful existence.

Fear of failure, perfectionism, and a lack of drive are the key contributors to procrastination. Negative and suffocating self-beliefs are at the heart of it. Some people just lack motivation, which causes them to put things off. They frequently put things off until the last minute. Even if they are aware that acting is in their best interests, they decide not to.

A procrastinator may do so out of fear of failing, making a mistake, receiving criticism, or just not being good enough. They may put things off because they think they need to be flawless in order to be accepted or approved of. They overthink and overplan. If someone tries to make everything perfect, they will never start. In actuality, the "mother of procrastination" is perfectionism. Those who procrastinate frequently need to understand and accept that failure is fine and that perfection is a question of perspective. Six practises of typical tardy people in the 21st century

- They check their emails every five minutes.
- They let their computer's news stream distract them.
- They update their phones with the newest apps.
- They watch their favourite movie on Netflix after reading their Facebook alerts.
- They look at their Twitter feed and Amazon to see what offers are available.
- People who procrastinate will make any excuse and use any delay strategy to avoid completing the task at hand.

Habits increase the automaticity of behavioural patterns. Take into account the fact that once we are experienced drivers, we no longer actively consider what we do every time we get in a car. Even more difficult routines, like going to the gym or studying a language, might develop stronger automaticity. That is accomplished by cuing and repetition.

Whatever sort of procrastinator you are, repeatedly putting off activities raises the risk of poor mental and physical health, according to experts. According to research, procrastination is linked to sleep issues like shorter sleep duration, a higher risk of insomnia symptoms, and excessive daytime drowsiness. Many people use "revenge bedtime procrastination," which is the propensity to put off going to bed in order to fit in personal activities.

Additionally, procrastination and cardiac issues are related. Sirois oversaw a 2015 study published in the Journal of Behavioral Medicine that discovered heart disease patients were more likely to self-identify as procrastinators than healthy individuals. The study found that procrastinators with hypertension and heart disease were less inclined to change their diets or exercise in order to manage their illnesses.

Develop compassion for yourself. People who procrastinate tend to be harsh on themselves. They could be ashamed of their own slowness or feel guilty about disappointing others. According to Sirois' research, procrastination and a lack of self-compassion are related. Treating oneself with compassion and empathy will help you combat it. I don't need to beat myself up," she added, simply admitting, "Yeah, maybe I messed up, and maybe I should have started sooner." I'm not the first person to put things off, and I won't be the last; tell yourself that. Self-compassion, according to Sirois, does not result in laziness. The opposite, she asserted, is true: "Research has shown that it really boosts people's drive to improve themselves."

It may come as no surprise that chronic procrastination, or having a tendency to put off tasks regularly over an extended period of time, has been linked to a number of detrimental mental and physical health outcomes, such as anxiety and depression, poor health conditions like the flu and colds, and even more serious conditions like cardiovascular disease.

Impulsive people are more prone to delay because they have a propensity to act on the immediate temptations that keep them from sitting down and getting started. As a result, especially if the work is far enough in the future, they veer off in a variety of directions other than the one that would lead to completion of the assignment. Another aspect of procrastination is self-regulation, or the capacity to organise and arrange your mental efforts. You must be able to participate in deliberate problem-solving in order to meet a deadline. This involves setting objectives, assessing your progress toward attaining those goals, and, if required, changing your approach.

You could be asking, "Where is the contradiction thus far?" Procrastinators may be genetically predisposed to the behaviour, may not give activities with distant deadlines much attention, and may avoid unpleasant chores. Additionally, they struggle more with organising their goal-setting techniques. There should be no surprises there. When we consider people's irrational beliefs—their ideas about their capacities that have no basis in reality and, in fact, can make things far worse—the paradox comes into play. Irrational beliefs have the potential to be cunning motivators for procrastination.

A self-handicapping or belief-based method, on the other hand, causes you to put off doing the activity until the very last minute. You feel unconsciously insufficient when presented with the work. Instead of allowing your failure to lower your self-esteem, you create a scenario that will ensure your failure, but you won't have to blame it on your incapability. You now have a valid defence in place: "I didn't have enough time." If you're attempting to maintain a shaky sense of self, this is far preferable to saying, "I didn't have enough skill."

There are several more reasons why people could self-handicap. Some people appear to almost want to fail because the idea of achievement threatens them. The Control Mastery Theory viewpoint contends that some of us would prefer failure because success would reflect poorly on other individuals who are important to us.

For instance, first-generation college students could experience an exaggerated sense of guilt about attending a school near their parents or other relatives. They erroneously think that if they are successful, they will harm their loved ones' reputations. As a result, they create roadblocks that prevent them from achieving their goals. They submit work that is hurried, lacking, or otherwise subpar.

Undoubtedly, some family members may feed their kids' illogical views and instil real shame in them. The student can be required to return home each time there is a "family emergency" (broadly defined). Due to the student's conflicting feelings, he or she finally gives in to remorse and is expelled from school. Some students, however, act on their own inner guilt even in the absence of clear family pressure and, ironically, disappoint their families.

Self-efficacy is low. Low self-efficacy , possibly more prevalent, irrational belief: the notion that you are not capable of doing a job. Low self-efficacy is more than simply a lack of confidence; it's a precise conviction that you are incapable of doing a certain kind of work. When assessing a person's self-efficacy, psychologists ask them to rank their chances of success at a particular task. It is possible to have great self-efficacy about your softball skills but poor self-efficacy about your public speaking skills. An overarching feeling of self-efficacy does not exist. Low self-efficacy might contribute to procrastination by making you delay a task because you don't believe you can get enough organised to do it.

Robert Klassen and colleagues from the University of Alberta's psychology department showed that students who had the lowest levels of self-efficacy to self-regulate were more prone to delay. Of the procrastinators, 25% thought that procrastination had the most detrimental impact on them.

The "negative procrastinators" were those who put off critical tasks longer, waited longer to start them, and actually received inferior marks. In contrast, "neutral procrastinators" spent more time procrastinating on less interesting jobs. Negative procrastinators struggle with self-management and strategy planning, which may reflect and contribute to their low self-efficacy and, ultimately, academic performance.

The fear that individuals feel when they teeter on the brink of missing crucial deadlines, however, is a third factor in the paradox of procrastination. This goes beyond the illogical assumption that working under pressure would make you more productive. Some people appear to have arousing inclinations when they experience the excitement of nearly failing to finish a task in time.

Although procrastination experts disagree on whether arousal-related procrastination can be distinguished from general procrastination. It appears that some people are more prone than others to procrastinating as a form of thrill-seeking. According to a study done in 2011 by psychologist Erin Freeman and colleagues at the University of Dallas, students who score highest on the extraversion scale are more likely to procrastinate out of arousal. Extraverts may require that surge of excitement to catapult them into the higher degree of arousal they need to do the activity successfully, in contrast to introverts, who often are more highly task-focused.

Another factor in the paradox of procrastination is the fear of making errors. Strongly perfectionistic individuals may finish their assignments on time but put off turning them in for review for as long as possible because they want to be sure that everything is flawless. This conduct is contradictory because these people run the risk of receiving negative feedback if they submit their projects late or not at all. Although they like it when work is submitted on time, managers also appreciate it when it is submitted early. Strong perfectionists behave no differently than less scrupulous people who squeeze in right before a deadline expires, according to their outward conduct.

Let's now discuss the categories of illogical ideas that might cause you to put off doing anything. Here's how you transform these crazy ideas into a timely blueprint: Deal with your fear of success. Consider the possibility that self-handicapping is preventing you from going all in to achieve your goals if you are constantly in danger of losing everything you have worked for. Dispel the notion that your loved ones don't want you to succeed since it's likely that they will celebrate your success.

Develop your ability to self-regulate. Are you certain that you won't be able to complete your tasks on time? Disappointed in your capacity to plan and prioritise your time? Focus on jobs that are due soon while you practise taking on minor activities that you know you can handle. When you can plan well, you may expand the range and time frame of your due dates, which will boost your confidence in yourself and your sense of accomplishment.

Other than delaying, find other methods to get your pleasures. Stop working with a deadline that is too close to danger. Focus your attention on the times you really made a mistake and got into trouble rather than recalling the times you escaped disaster by bringing your work in at the last minute. If you are aware that you are a terrible deadline pusher, you can force yourself to embrace your own, internally manufactured deadlines. You should eventually be able to spread those out over a longer period of time. Moderate perfectionism and a focus on action It's admirable to want to get the finest results, but not if doing so means losing out on opportunities or coming across as no more timely than careless procrastination. If you believe that you are unable to fight this inclination on your own, look for a work or study partner who excels at "locomotion" and can teach you how to concentrate on doing the task at hand efficiently.

No one can ever totally escape procrastination since it is such a universal human trait. You can, however, challenge the illogical assumptions that underpin chronic procrastination. Time can be on your side if you're prepared to question and alter these assumptions.

Every procrastinator has a vein of immature defiance running through them. You'd like to do something completely different from what you should be doing. And you'd much rather be involved in the exciting activity. Despite your best efforts and the knowledge in your somewhat grownup brain that the flashy, enjoyable item isn't the best use of your time, this still manages to happen.

Perfectionism appears to be the more covert and elusive of the two. How can you tell whether you are of the perfectionist school of thought? Because perfectionists frequently ignore the process in favour of the product, the outcomes had better be good.

Even though perfectionists are frequently excellent achievers, they never truly feel satisfied with their accomplishments because they think there is always more to do, be, and achieve. Perfectionists usually berate themselves for any minor mistakes they make since they are their own worst critics. Perfectionists frequently work in fits and spurts, starting out fiercely before succumbing to exhaustion.

This irrational pursuit of perfection results from efforts to uphold a feeling of self-worth that is dependent on the opinions of others. In light of the fact that perfection is impossible, it is frequently referred to as "the ultimate kind of self-abuse." More significantly, daily life and work seldom require perfection (unless you are a brain surgeon).

Procrastination is simple to recognise: Are you working on the tasks you want to do or are required to complete, or are you browsing the internet, reading Facebook postings, organising paperwork, doing laundry, or running errands? You are delaying if the latter question was answered in the affirmative. While identifying your preferred method of procrastination might be humorous, identifying the root of your procrastination is more crucial.

People tend to repeat the cycle despite the drawbacks of perfectionism and procrastination because it is what they are familiar with. The loop must be broken, though. You waste time beating yourself up psychologically by putting off chores that you agreed to do in the first place. And when I say "precious time," I mean it in the broadest sense possible—you only have so much time to live on Earth.

Do you truly want to write the proposal for a possible new customer instead of browsing through all of your friends' Facebook updates? The adversary of creativity, productivity, and sanity is perfectionism (and the procrastination that follows from it), which is another reason to stop the cycle. Perfectionists are victims of risk-averse thinking, which prevents invention and creativity because they are so focused on the end being flawless. Ironically, effective perfectionists and procrastinators are successful despite, not because of, their tendencies. Finally, procrastination and perfectionism both have long-term negative effects on one's mental and physical health. Perfectionism is a harmful way of thinking that frequently results in despair, self-doubt, and mental weariness.

Both procrastination and waiting do harm. Not only do procrastinators waste their valuable time, attention, and focus, but the ongoing stress that results from procrastinating eventually causes issues including weakened immunity, gastrointestinal issues, and sleeplessness.

If you procrastinate because you are afraid of failing, you can use some of the following action-based mind tactics to overcome fear: As you "get ready" to do it, pretend you're not going to. Instead of drafting the proposal, just make some notes to help you be ready to write it. While you're at it, you should probably start getting ready to write it by conducting a pertinent online search for supporting data. so on. The distinction between preparing to do something and actually doing it will eventually become fuzzier.

Put the most critical task at the head of the list and the other key tasks that need to be completed below it to practise organised procrastination. Even if you skip the most critical task and focus on the others, you will still complete vital tasks. Utilising the potential of what I like to refer to as "white space creativity" is another method of controlled procrastination. When doing mindless tasks like cleaning the dishes, gardening, or organising, good ideas frequently occur. The key is to use these hobbies as a means of idea generation rather than as a means of job avoidance.

Uncertainty is one of the main causes of procrastination since it tends to make tasks appear bigger and more difficult than they actually are. Procrastination may be prevented by developing a more accurate sense of time. Breaking down the seemingly impossible work into manageable chunks or bits is the first step.

Give yourself five or ten minutes to concentrate. For five to ten minutes, you can shoulder through anything, right? Breaking the siren call of putting it off and putting it off will put you on the path to finishing the assignment with even a little attention.

Procrastination is harmful, as everyone is aware. But being flawless is okay, right? Wrong. Both are challenging and frequently coexist, creating an endless cycle that may devastate both your productivity and your mental health. Perfectionism appears to be the more covert and elusive of the two. How can you tell whether you are of the perfectionist school of thought? Because perfectionists frequently ignore the process in favour of the product, the outcomes had better be good. Even though perfectionists are frequently excellent achievers, they never truly feel satisfied with their accomplishments because they think there is always more to do, be, and achieve.

Perfectionists usually berate themselves for any minor mistakes they make since they are their own worst critics.

Perfectionists frequently work in fits and spurts, starting out fiercely before succumbing to exhaustion. This irrational pursuit of perfection results from efforts to uphold a feeling of self-worth that is dependent on the opinions of others.

To be clear, procrastination does not equal indolence. It's more of a false feeling of activity born out of an inability to handle disappointment and failure. People use distraction to avoid discomfort when they see a greater difficulty than they feel capable of overcoming. According to studies, people delay when they see tangible jobs in an abstract way.

For example, if you put off doing something that appears to take a long time only to discover that it actually took less time than you anticipated, Procrastination is simple to recognise: Are you working on the tasks you want to do or are required to complete, or are you browsing the internet, reading Facebook postings, organising paperwork, doing laundry, or running errands? You are delaying if the latter question was answered in the affirmative. While identifying your preferred method of procrastination might be humorous, identifying the root of your procrastination is more crucial.

People tend to repeat the cycle despite the drawbacks of perfectionism and procrastination because it is what they are familiar with. The loop must be broken, though. You waste time beating yourself up psychologically by putting off chores that you agreed to do in the first place. And when I say "precious time," I mean it in the broadest sense possible—you only have so much time to live on Earth.

Do you truly want to write the proposal for a possible new customer instead of browsing through all of your friends' Facebook updates?

The adversary of creativity, productivity, and sanity is perfectionism (and the procrastination that follows from it), which is another reason to stop the cycle. Perfectionists are victims of risk-averse thinking, which prevents invention and creativity because they are so focused on the end being flawless. Ironically, effective perfectionists and procrastinators are successful despite, not because of, their tendencies.

Both procrastination and waiting do harm. Not only do procrastinators waste their valuable time, attention, and focus, but the ongoing stress that results from procrastinating eventually causes issues including weakened immunity, gastrointestinal issues, and sleeplessness.

Finally, procrastination and perfectionism both have long-term negative effects on one's mental and physical health. Perfectionism is a harmful way of thinking that frequently results in despair, self-doubt, and mental weariness.

CHAPTER TWO

Embracing Enkrateia: Be More Productive

"Procrastination frequently leads to bitter regret.The wisest course of action is to complete today's tasks in their appropriate order rather than putting them off until tomorrow."- Ida Scott Taylor.

As the opposite of akrasia, Aristotle created the term "enkrateia." While enkrateia implies being "in power over oneself," akrasia alludes to our propensity to succumb to procrastination. You may make it simpler to live an enkrateia-based life than an akrasia-based one by planning your future activities, lowering the difficulty of beginning positive habits, and employing implementation objectives.

Enkrateia, pronounced en-KRAH-tay-ah, is its antonym, according to Aristotle, and means "to be in control over oneself" and derives from possession or dominion over something or someone. We frequently experience anxiety because our brains have a propensity to place a larger value on present benefits than on future gains. But how can we get over it?

Enkrateia also derives from the Greek word enkratês, which means to own or have authority over. The human brain has a behavioural propensity to prefer current benefits over future ones. To empower yourself and embrace Enkrateia in order to accomplish your goals, you must reject Akrasia. Refer to the framework to overcome procrastination and establish new habits for long-term productivity in both your personal and professional lives.

Enkrateia is frequently described as "self-control," but "self-governance" is a far better term. The word democracy is derived from the root kratia, which implies governance (democracy, rule by the people; plutocracy, rule of the rich; etc.).

Enkrateia can be conceptualised psychologically as the formation or growth of a specialised sub-ego, an "inner governor" or "inner lawgiver," who governs the others. Contrary to common opinion, this concept is the subject of Plato's Republic, which used a physical city-state as a metaphor to comprehend the principles of inner self-governance rather than being primarily about how to construct an ideal political state.

Our brains favour short-term rewards above long-term gains. It is only a result of the way our thoughts operate. The fifteen-minute pattern Anthony Trollope once penned more than 40 books, which were created by James Clear. Procrastination boosts goal-setting productivity. Anthony Trollope published a staggering amount of work, beginning with his debut novel in 1847. He authored 47 novels, 18 nonfiction books, 12 short stories, 2 plays, and a variety of essays and correspondence throughout the course of the following 38 years. Trollope wrote for three hours a day, in 15-minute chunks, to accomplish his astounding output.

Anthony Trollope worked as a book author, and producing a book is a significant undertaking. You cannot finish this kind of work in a single day. Sometimes the effort of simply writing a chapter is too much to handle in one day. Trollope, on the other hand, measured his progress in 15-minute increments rather than by the completion of chapters or volumes. Because of this method, he was able to continue working on the challenging process of producing a book while immediately experiencing emotions of fulfilment and achievement.

"At this point, it had been my habit—and it still is, though lately I've been a little more tolerant of myself—to write with my watch in front of me and set a goal of 250 words every 15 minutes."- Anthony Trollope

Long-term momentum is maintained by taking little steps, which increases your likelihood of completing challenging activities. Your day will take on a more proactive and effective attitude the faster you finish productive tasks. In addition, Anthony Trollope didn't have to wait three days or three months to finish a chapter in order to have a feeling of success. He was able to monitor his development every fifteen minutes. He could mentally cross off that time block from his list and feel instantly successful if he completed 250 words.

Trollope's 15-minute writing sessions served as a clever progress gauge that helped him accomplish a significant assignment more quickly. He realised the long-term benefits of focusing on the most crucial tasks and the short-term benefits of accomplishing each tiny time block without delay.

The largest shipbuilder and second-largest steel manufacturer in America at the time, Bethlehem Steel Corporation, was led by Schwab as president. Thomas Edison, a well-known inventor, allegedly called Schwab the "master hustler." He was always looking for a way to beat the competition. In 1918, Schwab set up a meeting with renowned productivity expert Ivy Lee in an effort to improve the productivity of his workforce and find more effective ways to complete tasks. Lee is regarded as a pioneer in the area of public relations and was a successful businessman in his own right. According to the legend, Lee was summoned into Schwab's office and instructed to "Show me a method to get more things done."

Lee said, "Give me 15 minutes with each of your executives."

Schwab inquired, "How much would it cost me?"

Lee answered nothing. Unless it functions, you can write me a check after three months for as much as you think it's worth to you.

Ivy Lee spent 15 minutes with each executive explaining his straightforward daily practise for maximising productivity: List the six most crucial tasks you have to complete tomorrow at the conclusion of each workday. Put no more than six items on your list. Put those six things in order of their real significance.

Keep your attention solely on the first assignment when you come tomorrow. Before beginning the second task, complete the first one first. Apply the same strategy to the remaining items on your list. Any work left undone at the end of the day should be added to a fresh list of six assignments for the next day. Every working day, repeat this procedure. It appears ridiculously easy to prioritise your to-do list using the Ivy Lee Method. How could something so basic be so valuable?

It is straightforward enough to function. The main criticism of approaches like this one is that they are very simplistic. They don't take into consideration all the subtleties and complexity of life. What transpires in the event of an emergency? How about maximising the benefits of the most recent technology? In my opinion, complexity is frequently a flaw since it makes it more difficult to get back on track. Yes, there will be unforeseen situations and distractions. Ignore them as much as you can, deal with them when necessary, and return as quickly as you can to your priority to-do list. Simple guidelines can help direct complicated behavior. It forces you to make difficult choices. I don't think Lee's advice to complete six vital chores each day is really amazing. Five chores per day is also an option. But I do believe that setting boundaries for oneself has a special power. Pruning your ideas and eliminating everything that isn't absolutely required is, in my experience, the greatest thing to do when you have too many ideas or when you're feeling overwhelmed by all you need to get done.

Lee's approach is comparable to Warren Buffett's "25-5 Rule," which mandates that you concentrate only on 5 essential activities while ignoring everything else. In essence, if you don't commit to anything, everything will divert your attention. It eliminates starting-related resistance. Starting most projects is the largest obstacle to completing them.

With Lee's approach, you must choose your first assignment the evening before reporting for duty. As a writer, I may spend three to four hours discussing what I should write about on any given day, so this technique has been tremendously helpful for me. However, if I make a decision the previous evening, I may get up and begin writing right away. It's straightforward, yet it functions. Starting is just as important as succeeding at all.

We can always persuade ourselves we'd have done a better job if we had more time." Procrastination is a means for us to be content with subpar outcomes. This is a cheap way to be happy, but if you're excellent at justifying, you can keep yourself feeling somewhat fulfilled. Your expectations of yourself are getting progressively lower.

You must focus on one thing at a time. Today's culture is all about multitasking. The fallacy of multitasking is the idea that being busy equates to superior performance. It is true—exactly the opposite. Work gets done better when there are fewer priorities. Study top professionals in almost every industry, including sports, artists, scientists, teachers, and CEOs, and you'll find that they all share one trait in common: attention. It's easy to understand why. If you consistently split your time 10 ways, you cannot excel at any one activity. Focus and consistency are necessary for mastery.

Around 2006, two Harvard professors started researching the causes of procrastination. Even when it seems obvious that doing the right thing is in our best interests, why do we resist doing it?

The two academics, Todd Rogers and Max Bazerman, asked research participants whether they would agree to sign up for a savings plan that would automatically deposit two percent of their income into a savings account in order to find out the response to this question. The majority of participants thought it was a good idea to save money, but their actions suggested otherwise:

In one question variant, participants were urged to sign up for the savings plan as soon as possible. Only 30% of respondents said that they would be willing to sign up for the plan in this case.

Another variation of the question urged participants to sign up for a savings plan in the future (like a year from today). 77% of respondents said that they would agree to sign up for the plan in this case.

Spending money now has an immediate benefit (a new iPhone!). But neglecting to prepare for retirement has a long-term penalty that won't become apparent until you're years behind. Unrestricted fossil fuel use has an immediate return (more energy, heat, and power!), whereas the cost of climate change won't become apparent until decades after the harm has been done.

However, our decisions typically shift when we think about these issues in the far future. Which would you prefer in a year: being healthy and regularly exercising, or being overweight and eating donuts? The decision is simple in the long run, but when it comes to making it right now, we underestimate the short-term advantages of engaging in unproductive habits and undervalue their long-term costs.

When we think about the future, we want to make decisions that lead to long-term benefits ("Yes, I'll save more!"), but when we think about the present, we want to make decisions that lead to short-term benefits ("I'll spend it right now," etc.). Behavioral economists call this concept "time inconsistency."

The Present You vs. Future You dilemma is what I prefer to refer to it as. Future You is aware that you should make decisions that will benefit you most in the long run, but

Present You has a propensity to place too much weight on actions that will benefit you immediately.

But everyone of us has the ability to regain control over our time and productivity. In the midst of our constantly connected lives, the pinging of our phones, and our increasingly hectic schedules, we've justlost sight of it.

To overcome procrastination and make better long-term decisions, you must discover a means to influence your current self to behave in your future self's best interests. Make procrastination's costs more apparent right away. Eliminate any environmental factors that can cause procrastination.

I've found that prioritising tasks according to their actual relevance and completing the most crucial tasks first produce the best outcomes for me in terms of getting things done. This is the ideal approach, in my opinion, since it compels you to focus your efforts on the activities that are most important.

If the top duty is a fairly large project, after rating your priorities for the day, you may become dissatisfied because it takes a long time to finish. For instance, I worked on a project last week that took two days to finish. I started the assignment on Tuesday morning, knowing I wouldn't be able to finish it that day. By mid-afternoon, despite the fact that I knew I would work all day without finishing the assignment, I was still feeling frustrated. I had spent the entire day working on the most crucial duty, but all I had to show for it was an incomplete project when it was 4 p.m. Even though I was using my time well, my to-do list remained as lengthy as it was in the morning.

Make long-term behaviour more immediately rewarded. Our need for an instant reward is what causes us to put things off. Procrastination may be avoided if you can discover a means to make the advantages of wise long-term decisions more apparent right away.

Simple visualisation of the advantages your future self will experience is one method for doing this. Imagine how much better your life will be if you manage to save money. Consider the benefits of saving money for the future. In your mind's eye, bring the reward from the future into the present.

Highlight the direct consequences of procrastination. You can be made to pay the price of procrastination in many different ways, and sooner rather than later. For instance, skipping your workout the next week won't have much of an effect on your life if you exercise alone. You won't see an instant decline in health as a result of skipping that one workout. Only after weeks or months of being inactive does exercising become painfully expensive.

However, the expense of skipping your workout becomes more apparent if you make a prior commitment to working out with a friend at 7 a.m. on Monday. If you skip this workout, you'll come out as rude.

Eliminate procrastination-inducing elements from your surroundings. Changing your surroundings is the most effective approach to altering your behaviour.

It doesn't take much speculation to determine why this is the case. In a typical circumstance, you could decide to opt for a cookie over a serving of veggies. What if the cookie never materialised in the first place? Making the proper decision is much simpler if there are superior options all around you. Eliminate any distractions from your surroundings and design a room with better architectural choices.

Our world is ultimately defined by these everyday decisions. The distractions we avoid are increasingly determining our ability to achieve.

We have to make many little judgements every day. the choice between giving in to temptation and embracing rapid satisfaction or resisting it and committing to a long-term activity.

If you get to perform one of your favourite activities while engaging in a habit, you're more likely to find it appealing. Perhaps you want to learn about the most recent celebrity rumors, but you need to get in shape.

One approach to using Premack's Principle, a psychological theory, is to bundle temptations. The principle asserts that "more probable activities will reinforce less probable behaviours," taking its name from professor David Premack's study. To put it another way, even if you don't really want to process past-due work emails, you'll train yourself to do it if it means you'll get to do something else along the way that you actually want to do.

List your favourite pastimes and your strongest temptations in column one. List the actions and behaviours you ought to be engaging in but frequently put off in column two. Spend some time noting as many behaviours as you can. Next, go over your list to see if you can connect any of your "desire" actions with things you "should" be doing.

"Every man ought to be awakened to the active pursuit of whatever he is eager to do. Life cannot be lengthy, and it is probable that it will be far shorter than nature permits. Although success cannot be guaranteed by effort and even the fastest career can be cut short by death, a person who is killed while carrying out an honourable task at least has the honour of falling in rank and having participated in the struggle, even if he doesn't come out on top."- Smith Johnson

There are numerous things that affect performance, but you can make a compelling case that the one skill that sets top achievers apart from everyone else is the capacity to regularly complete activities that are essential but not urgent. Think about all the duties that are necessary for our advancement but are not urgent in our everyday lives. Even though working out regularly won't feel essential on any one day, doing so will improve both your health and your quality of life. Because of temptation bundling, it's simple to complete these tasks that are always necessary but never feel urgent. By letting your vices draw you in, you might make it simpler to stick with more challenging routines that have long-term benefits.

Sir Isaac Newton's mathematical principles of natural philosophy, a ground-breaking work, in 1687. It contained a description of his three principles of motion. In the process, Newton reshaped how people saw physics and science and laid the groundwork for classical mechanics. The three principles of motion described by Newton may serve as an excellent parallel for boosting productivity, streamlining tasks, and generally enhancing your life, which is something that most people are unaware of. I'd like to describe this comparison as being based on Newton's Laws of Productivity.

Newton's First Law Of Productivity

Unless acted upon by an external force, an object either stays at rest or keeps moving at a constant speed. (Or, things moving tend to keep moving.(Things at rest frequently remain at rest.) Procrastination is, in many respects, a universal principle. It's the first Newtonian law to be applied to production. Things that are at rest frequently stay at rest. Things in motion usually continue to move. This only implies one thing when it comes to being productive: finding a method to start is crucial. Maintaining motion is considerably simpler once you get going. The physics of productivity's first law can help you increase your output. So, what is the ideal method to begin when you are unable to stop postponing?

You might not feel like running right now. However, if you put on your running shoes and fill up your water bottle, that little beginning can be plenty to get you outside. You can be writing your paper right now while gazing at a blank screen. However, if you write incoherently for only two minutes, you could discover that valuable phrases begin to flow from your fingertips. You could be having a creativity block right now and finding it difficult to create anything. However, if you turn a random line on a piece of paper into a dog, you could spark your imagination. Motivation frequently surfaces after beginning. Try to start off modestly. Things in motion usually continue to move.

Newton's Second Law of Productivity

F=ma is the second law of motion. The product of an object's mass and its acceleration vector is the vector sum of the forces acting on that object. (For example, mass times acceleration equals force.) Let's examine F=ma in more detail and see how it relates to productivity.

In this equation, there is something crucial to keep in mind. A vector represents the force, F. Both magnitude (how much labour you are putting in) and direction are included in vectors (where that work is focused). To put it another way, if you wish to accelerate an item in a specific direction, both the size and the direction of the force you apply will matter. What's this? The same holds true for accomplishing goals in your life.

It's important to consider where your effort is applied in addition to how hard you work (in terms of magnitude) if you want to be productive (direction). This is true for both significant life decisions and ordinary daily choices. For instance, using the same skill set in several ways might produce quite diverse outcomes. The physics of productivity's first law can help you increase your output.

Newton's Third Law of Productivity:

When one body applies a force to another, the second body responds by applying a force to the first body that is both equal in strength and directed in the opposite direction. (That is, opposing and equal forces.) Each of us operates in life at a certain average speed. Similar to Newton's equal and opposing forces, your average levels of productivity and efficiency are frequently a balance of the productive and unproductive factors in your life.

In our lives, there are positive energies like motivation, positivism, and focus. Additionally, there are unproductive factors like stress, sleep deprivation, and attempting to handle too many activities at once. The third law of the physics of productivity can help you increase your output.

There are two options available to us if we wish to increase our effectiveness and productivity. The addition of additional productive forces is the first option. The "power through it" approach is this. We endure it, savour another cup of coffee, and continue working. This is why some people take medications to help them focus or watch a movie to motivate themselves.All of this is done in an effort to boost your productive force and defeat the counterproductive forces that exist. The third law of the physics of productivity can help you increase your output.

Obviously, you can only maintain this level of effort for so long before you become exhausted, but for a little while, the "power through it" approach can be effective. The second choice is to defeat the adversarial forces. Reduce the quantity of duties you take on, simplify your life, develop the ability to say "no," alter your surroundings, and do whatever else is necessary to overcome the obstacles in your path. The third law of the physics of productivity can help you increase your output.

Your productivity will increase organically if you decrease the counterproductive elements in your life. It's as though the hand that has been restraining you vanishes mysteriously. (As I like to say, you wouldn't need productivity suggestions if you got rid of everything that was keeping you from being productive.) Most individuals try to push through the obstacles and force their way beyond them. The issue with this tactic is that you are still dealing with the opposing force. Eliminating the competing pressures and letting production advance organically makes me feel a lot less stressed.

Using Newton's principles of motion, you may learn pretty much all there is to know about how to be productive. Things in motion usually continue to move. Find a technique to start the process in under two minutes. Working on the correct things is just as important as working hard. You can only use so much force, and where you use it counts.

An equilibrium of competing forces determines your production. You have two options if you want to be more productive: push through the obstacles or get rid of the opposing forces. The second choice appears to be less demanding.

We frequently believe that being productive entails doing more tasks each day. Wrong. Being productive means constantly completing vital tasks. There are just a few things that are actually vital, regardless of what you are working on. Being productive requires doing a few things at a steady, average pace rather than everything at top speed.

This is the reason this tactic works. You'll always accomplish something significant if you start each day by doing what is most essential. Unknown to you, this is a significant event for me. On many days, I spend hours checking off the fourth, fifth, or sixth most crucial items on my to-do list but never really get around to performing the most crucial thing.

Your willpower will be depleted if you keep making decisions. This is true even if you make the same little choice over and over again, such as restraining yourself from checking your email. (An additional illustration would be striving to adhere to a rigorous diet every day.) Your resolve may allow you to resist for five minutes, an hour, or even a week, but ultimately it will wear down, and you'll cave. Decision fatigue is what causes this, and I previously wrote about how it has an appreciable effect on your willpower and the decisions you make each day.

Many people express a desire for choices. However, having alternatives isn't necessarily a good thing when it comes to getting things done. Making the proper decision actually gets more difficult when everything is an option (or any choice at all).

You might choose to consume only one kind of vegetable this week if you wish to eat more veggies. By restricting your options, you'll be more likely to actually eat something healthy rather than becoming stressed out trying to figure out every last element of the ideal diet. We frequently believe that we desire an open road and the freedom to go in whatever direction we like. However, there are occasions when we require a tunnel that will narrow our options and point us in a certain direction.

However, contrasting your existing circumstance with that of a successful person might frequently leave you feeling as though you lack the means to even begin. It may be quite simple to persuade yourself that you need to acquire new possessions, acquire new skills, or meet new people before you can even begin moving toward your objectives if you consider their ideal setup.

Using the excuse that you need to "learn more" or "get your ducks in a row" as a crutch might keep you from making progress on the things that are really important.

You can whine that you need new clubs and that this is why your game is deteriorating, but in reality, all you really need is two years of practise. You may counter that it's challenging to travel light without the proper bag, but in reality, you could manage with what you now have. You can highlight the fact that your business mentor uses XYZ software as a reason for their success, but chances are they didn't start out using it. It might be shrewd to avoid doing hard work by obsessing about the best diet, golf club, strategy, or other aspect of your life. Regular readers are aware that I support optimisation and improvement. Gains of one percent make me happy. Small routines captivate me. Consistency at disturbing levels makes my heart race. But don't let ideas of the ideal stop you from starting in the first place.

You shouldn't wait to start just because you don't like where you have to start. I wish I had started off as a better writer. I regret not starting out as a more savvy businessperson. I wish I had more skill with a camera when I picked one up. But more than anything, I'm pleased I made the decision to begin, despite the fact that I wasn't very good at first. You tend to feel underprepared when you're experiencing feelings of anxiety and uncertainty.

Who says you won't succeed? You won't necessarily get hired just because someone else was turned down for the position. Even if the publisher doesn't like your friend's novel, they may still publish it. It's possible that you've attempted weight loss in the past, but that doesn't mean you can't achieve it again. You won't always "miss that lift." You could even be destined for success. Stop acting as though failure is guaranteed. It isn't.

Not taking any action at all is the only genuine failure. We all experience dread, apprehension, and vulnerability. And regrettably, the majority of us let those emotions guide our behaviour. Because of this, your ability to act is frequently what sets you apart from the majority of individuals. You only need to be the one person who makes the decision to really do it; you don't need to be excellent at what you do. By taking action on the things that most people find reasons to put off, you may achieve great achievement.

Athletes, singers, CEOs, and artists are all top achievers who consistently outperform their counterparts. While everyone else struggles to stay motivated and is constantly weighed down by the demands of daily life, they consistently show up and produce. After a poor performance, a lousy workout, or just a bad day at work, most individuals get demotivated and lose focus, whereas great performers return to their routine immediately the next day.

How do you live a healthy life? is the key issue that unites our community, and it is what I attempt to write about every Monday and Thursday. Along with proper diet and exercise, this also entails travel and adventure, artistic expression, and community engagement.

But consistency is necessary regardless of the subject at hand. Whatever your idea of a "healthy life" is, you'll need to overcome procrastination if you want to really live it. The Seinfeld Strategy should help put the conflict in perspective. Maintaining a consistent training schedule can help you get fit more rapidly. You'll notice that results arrive considerably faster in your business if you don't break the chain. Keep up the momentum in your artistic endeavours, and you'll discover that you'll consistently generate original stuff.

Control your energy rather than your time. You'll probably come to the realisation that you perform specific activities better at particular times if you give it some thought. For instance, I write best in the morning since that is when I feel most creative. In contrast, I set aside my afternoons for meetings, calls, and emails. That is the best time for me to finish those tasks because I don't need much creative energy. And I find that I work out best in the late afternoon or early evening, so I go to the gym then. How do you feel when you first wake up? What activity calls for that energy the most?

We frequently believe that attaining excellence necessitates enormous effort and that our lofty objectives necessitate enormous amounts of desire and determination. But in reality, all we want is commitment to little, doable activities. Consistency leads to mastery. Create a list of minor victories to help you beat stress and worry. By getting rid of your self-imposed limitations, you may overcome your fear of acting. Build your surroundings to be clutter- and decision-fatigue-free. Prioritise your work by concentrating on finishing just one thing each day. Interrupting abrupt "impulse snaps" can help you train your brain to manage focus.

Get ready the previous evening. If you just accomplish one thing every day, spend a few minutes each night arranging your to-do list for the next day. I don't do this nearly as frequently as I should. When I do it correctly, I'll outline the piece I'll write the next day and create a list of the top priorities for me to complete. That evening, it takes 10 minutes, but the following day, it saves 3 hours.

Wait until noon to check your email. Sounds easy. It's never done. I had to fight the impulse to check my inbox for a long time before I understood that everything could wait a few hours. In the early morning hours of each day, don't check your email since no one is likely to send you an email concerning a genuine emergency (a death in the family, etc.). Instead of responding to what is "urgent," use the morning to do what is important.

Switch off your phone and put it in a different room. or on the desk of a coworker. Put it out of sight, or at the absolute least, hide it. This reduces the need to check Facebook, Twitter, Instagram, and other social media. By using this straightforward technique, you may avoid engaging in half-work, when you squander time shifting your focus between pointless things.

Work in a cool environment. Have you ever noticed how a heated environment makes you feel sleepy and lethargic? Focusing your mind and body is simple and may be accomplished by lowering the temperature or relocating to a colder location.

Stand or sit up. For your mind to function correctly, it needs oxygen. In order to supply your body with enough oxygen, your lungs must be able to expand and contract. That seems easy enough, but here's the issue: the majority of people sit slumped over and stare at a screen while typing. Your diaphragm presses against the bottom of your lungs, and your chest collapses while you are slumped over, making it difficult for you to breathe comfortably and deeply. You'll discover that you can breathe easier and more deeply if you sit up straight or stand up. Your brain will receive more oxygen as a consequence, which will improve your ability to focus.

Create a morning routine that serves as your "pre-game." I start my morning by pouring a glass of cold water. Some folks meditate for five minutes in the morning. Similar to that, you have to have a set order for your morning routine. Your brain receives a signal from this short pattern that it is time to start working, exercising, or going through whatever other mode you need to be in to complete your assignment. A pre-game ritual also assists you in overcoming a lack of motivation and doing tasks even when you don't feel like it.

It's uncommon for someone to achieve sudden success, just as it's uncommon for our lives to end abruptly. The majority of harmful or unproductive behaviours are the outcome of small, recurring decisions that develop into negative habits. This was a morning squandered. There was a fruitless morning there. The good news is that making consistent everyday decisions also yields remarkable outcomes. This is especially true of your morning routine. Frequently, how you begin the day determines how you end it.

People frequently believe it's strange to become excited about something as small as reading one page, sitting in silence for one minute, or making one sales call. But doing just one thing is not the purpose. The goal is to develop the habit of showing up. In actuality, a habit must be formed before it can be strengthened. You have little chance of understanding the more intricate concepts if you can't grasp the fundamental ability of showing up. Do the simple thing more frequently rather than striving to create a flawless habit from scratch. Before you can optimise, you must standardise. The initial two minutes merely become a ritual at the start of a broader routine as you develop the art of showing up. This is the best technique to learn a challenging skill, not just a trick to make habits easier. The more you ritualise the beginning of a process, the easier it will be to enter the deep attention required to accomplish great things. It is easier to achieve top performance when you warm up the same way before each activity. You may make it simpler to start the difficult job of producing by sticking to a routine.

You may make it simpler to go to bed at a decent hour each night by forming a reliable power-down habit. Even if you can't automate the entire procedure, you can make the initial step mindless. Make the initial steps simple, and the rest will follow.

To some, the Two-Minute Rule may appear to be a deception. Even if you are aware that going beyond the two-minute mark is the true objective, it could seem as though you are deceiving yourself. Nobody truly aspires to open their notes, read one page, or perform one push-up. Why would you fall for a mental trick if you were aware of it?

Time management is not always easy. There are frequently significant differences between what is important in your life and what is urgent. This is especially true when it comes to your health, since, despite the fact that your life ultimately depends on it, the crucial concerns nearly never feel urgent.

No, it is not vital for you to work out today, but it is crucial for your long-term health. No, you won't pass away from stress today, but you may if you don't work it out soon. No, eating whole, unadulterated foods will not make you live longer, but it will reduce your risk of developing diseases such as cancer.

It's ridiculously simple to divide our focus between what we should be doing and what society constantly distracts us from in today's world of continual distraction. The majority of the time, we are juggling our to-do lists with the demands of our messages, emails, and to-do lists. We rarely give the task at hand our entire attention.

You begin writing a paper but pause mid-sentence to check your phone or access Facebook or Twitter. You test out a brand-new exercise regimen. You learn about another "new" exercise regimen two days later and give it a go. In neither programme do you make any progress, so you begin looking for something better. While you're talking to someone on the phone, your thoughts start to stray to your email.

No matter where or how you fall into the half-work trap, the outcome is always the same: you never give a task your whole attention, you seldom devote yourself to a task for significant periods of time, and it takes you twice as long to complete half as much.

You accomplish more on the final day before a vacation (when you truly concentrate) than you do in the two weeks prior (when you're continuously distracted) because of half-work. Like most people, I always struggle with this issue, and the best solution I've discovered to cope with it is to set aside a large amount of time to dedicate to just one project while ignoring everything else. I choose one activity and dedicate the entire workout to it. Today is only for squats, for example. Anything additional is extra.

I set aside a few hours (or maybe a whole workday) to devote to a crucial assignment. I'll turn off my email, Facebook, and Twitter and leave my phone in another room. The only method I've found to enter into deep, concentrated work and prevent fragmented periods when you're only producing half-work is to completely eliminate distractions.

How much more could you accomplish if you completed the task you needed to do in the manner you needed to do it and stopped spending much of your time half-working and half-wandering?

As your day goes on, disorder and turmoil seem to get worse. The choices and decisions you make during the day also have a tendency to deplete your willpower. At the end of the day, your chances of making a wise choice are lower than they were in the morning. This same pattern has also been observed in my exercises, I've discovered. The harder I try to finish sets, grind out repetitions, and do challenging exercises, the less willpower I have.

I try my best to make sure that if there is something essential that I need to accomplish, I do it first for all of the aforementioned reasons. I have a glass of water and start typing as soon as I wake up if I have a big piece to write. I always start each workout with a challenging exercise if I need to do one.

If you do the most crucial tasks first, there will never be a day when you don't accomplish anything crucial.

Even if things don't go according to plan, you can typically have a productive day by using this straightforward technique. It is the only productivity advice you'll ever need: do the most crucial task first each day.

I've talked in the past about how important it is to hold oneself to a timetable rather than a deadline. There may be times when deadlines are appropriate, but I'm confident that sticking to a timetable is considerably more productive when it comes to completing crucial tasks over the long haul.

But sticking to a schedule might be difficult when it comes to the daily grind. Anyone who plans to exercise every Monday, Wednesday, and Friday will be able to tell you how difficult it is to consistently follow their routine.

I've made a slight change in how I approach my schedule to combat unforeseen diversions and the propensity to become sidetracked. In contrast to how we often approach our goals, my objective is to prioritise the timetable above the scope.

For instance, suppose you planned to run 3 kilometres this afternoon when you got up today. Your schedule became chaotic during the day, and you saw that time was passing quickly. You now have just 20 minutes left to work out. You now have a choice between two alternatives. The first is to decide that you don't have enough time to exercise today and use your remaining free time to work on anything else. In the past, I would have typically done this.

The second choice is to narrow the scope while maintaining the timeline. You run one mile, perform five sprints, or perform 30 jumping jacks in place of the usual three miles. But regardless of what, you keep to your routine and work out. Compared to the previous method, I have had far more long-term success using this one. Five sprints every day won't have much of an impact, especially if you were planning to run three kilometers. But consistently keeping to a schedule has a significant overall influence. No matter the situation or how brief the workout, you are confident that you will complete today's assignment. Little ambitions become lifelong habits in this way.

Finish something today, even if it's smaller than you thought it would be.

Numerous productivity tools and time-management applications are available. There are more calendars, to-do lists, and reminders than you can possibly use. But from my experience, the most useful and applicable time management advice is straightforward. Perhaps you've trained your entire life and are looking for a new activity to keep things interesting. Or perhaps you're starting to exercise for the first time and are unsure of how to get started. Regardless, establishing a new exercise regimen is something we all struggle with occasionally.

I've already discussed the value of having a sense of purpose, and the same is true with training and exercise. It will be simpler for you to train for success if you are more clear about what you want to get good at. In my instance, I wish to improve my 400-meter sprinting. That is a specific objective that gives me guidance throughout the process. Make a choice if you're unsure about how to begin exercising. It's not even necessary for it to be the "best" choice. Simply decide what it is that you want to excel at, then take steps to achieve that goal. Later on, there will be plenty of time for modifications and optimisation.

The majority of the time, we start a new exercise regimen because we are inspired to do so. Although having motivation is wonderful, it can also be a double-edged sword, as I've previously noted. Why? Initially, since motivation changes, you cannot rely on it because of this. You should thus focus on creating positive habits rather than finding motivation. However, motivation may sometimes deceive you into taking on more than you can handle. (I wrote here about why this is a problem and how to prevent it.) You should begin slowly at first. Remember that the goal is to develop a routine of exercise, not to engage in strenuous exercise.

The only thing standing between our actions and the outcomes we seek is often our commitment to carrying them out.

Start right away. "Until one is committed, there is hesitation and the potential to back away." One fundamental reality about all acts of initiative (and invention) prevents innumerable brilliant ideas and plans from coming to fruition: when one firmly commits, Providence also moves. Things of all kinds come about that would never have happened otherwise. The choice triggers a cascade of circumstances that bring about a variety of unexpected occurrences, meetings, and material help that no one could have imagined would occur in their favour.

"Start doing whatever you can or want to. Boldness possesses genius, strength, and magic. Do it right now."- W. H. Murray

We all have urgent duties to complete every day, such as answering a phone call, responding to an email, or providing assistance to a sick friend. However, by having a clear purpose and objective in mind, you can return to the essential activities right away after handling the urgent tasks of the day. A clear objective offers you focus and keeps you from getting caught in a flurry of time-consuming, pointless activity.

Never will anything worthwhile feel urgent. Significant goals are, by their nature, important. They no longer scream for attention. They demand long-term stability, a sense of direction, and a feeling of purpose. I suggest that we stop allowing the potential for greatness to elude us. I contend that we should stop the mad dash to mediocrity and begin the steady march to excellence.

It's more vital to have the guts to start than it is to succeed, since only those who continuously start something are capable of finishing it.

Despite what most individuals may claim, procrastinating seldom involves being lazy. When we delay, we frequently work furiously for extended periods of time right before our deadlines. Laziness is the antithesis of hard work; therefore, it can't be why we put in the effort. What causes us to put things off, and more importantly, what can we do to stop it?

Some claim they postpone because they are lazy, as was previously indicated. Others assert that they "work best" under pressure and "perform better" when they put things off. I urge you to evaluate and meditate on these justifications. Almost everyone who says this routinely puts off doing anything and hasn't finished a significant academic job that required planning, execution, evaluation, etc. before the due date. Therefore, they are unable to compare the situations in which they perform best. You can't really say you "perform better" under pressure if you pretty much always put off starting your duties and never actually go about them methodically. Others claim they like the "rush" of doing tasks quickly and meeting deadlines. They usually say things like that when they aren't under pressure.

In practically every day of our lives, we have times when we get a glimpse of who we are, what we're capable of, what we're meant to be, or what we want to be.

When they have forgotten the bad effects of procrastination, such as emotions of worry and tension, weariness, and disappointment from falling short of their own expectations and having to put their lives on hold for extended periods of time, they claim that this works before or after cramming. Not to mention, waiting until the last minute greatly increases the likelihood that something will go wrong, such as falling sick or having a computer malfunction, and you won't be able to get the necessary grade. Thus, delaying tasks might be difficult for us and actually raise the likelihood that we will fail, yet we still do it. Why is that?

Additionally, procrastination is not just a result of having bad time management abilities; it also has deeper, more intricate psychological causes.In schools where students are continuously evaluated, especially in colleges where there is a lot riding on students‘ success, these dynamics are frequently made worse. In actuality, students' procrastination is frequently a form of self-defense. For instance, if you put off doing anything, you can always use the justification that you "didn't have enough" time, which ensures that your confidence in your abilities is never in jeopardy. It makes sense that students would want to put off their work when there is so much pressure to achieve a decent score on, say, a paper.

The majority of the time, we postpone and avoid things out of dread and anxiety—fear of failing, fear of succeeding too well, fear of losing control, fear of seeming foolish, fear of having one's sense of self or self-concept questioned. To avoid having our talents scrutinised, we avoid performing labor. And if we do succeed, it makes us feel even "smarter." So what can we do to combat our procrastination tendencies?

To stop procrastinating, you must first understand why you do it and what purpose it serves in your life. If you don't fully comprehend the cause of the issue, you can't come up with a workable remedy. The secret to learning how to quit procrastinating is awareness and self-knowledge, just like with other difficulties. For many people, seeing how procrastination shields them from feeling inadequate and remembering this when they are tempted to relapse into old, fruitless postponing patterns goes a long way toward curing the issue.

Life is not a practise run. Everyone gains by taking the stage, even if only one person actually lives in the spotlight.

Time management strategies and tools are essential for overcoming procrastination, but they are insufficient on their own. Additionally, not all time management techniques work equally well for overcoming procrastination. Some time-management strategies can help you beat procrastination, while others can actually make it worse. The most effective ones are those that lessen fear and anxiety while highlighting the joy and benefits of doing activities. Inflexible people, those who highlight how big the jobs are, and people who make people more anxious might actually make them procrastinate more, which is counterproductive. Making a long list of "things to do" or arranging every hour of your day, for example, may raise your stress levels and lead to procrastination.

Instead, allow yourself flexibility, split up large chores into smaller ones, create acceptable goals (such as a doable list of things to accomplish), and designate time to activities you like as incentives for jobs completed.

You must continue to be motivated for productive reasons if you want to conquer procrastination. When I use the term "productive reasons," I mean motivations for learning and achievement that result in happy, fruitful, and fulfilling thoughts and behaviors. These motivations stand in contrast to doing something out of a sense of obligation to "show off," out of a desire to avoid upsetting your parents, out of a desire to avoid seeming foolish, or out of a desire to avoid failing. All of these are valid reasons—and sometimes very strong ones—for taking action, but they are ineffective because they frequently elicit unhelpful, unfavourable thoughts and behaviors. For instance, if you worry about appearing foolish, you could refrain from asking questions, exploring unfamiliar territory, utilising novel techniques, or taking the risks required to advance your knowledge and abilities. Setting and concentrating on objectives is an excellent method to get positive motives in action. Write out your individual motivations for enrolling in the course, and use a goal-setting chart to track your progress. Keep your motivation and objectives in mind. The objectives of other people for you are more duties than objectives. Being engaged and active will keep you motivated.

Maintaining active participation in your lessons is another strategy for combating procrastination. Your motivation will be weakened if you behave passively in class since you are probably not "getting into" the subject matter of the course. Additionally, if you are passive, it's likely that you are not getting the most out of the course and its contents. Nonsense and ambiguity are not interesting; on the contrary, they are dull and annoying. Something that is tedious or annoying is seldom something we want to accomplish. Avoid this by making it your goal to comprehend the information thoroughly rather than simply remember it or "get through it."

Concentrate on what you want to accomplish rather than what you want to avoid. By establishing for yourself positive, tangible, and relevant learning and accomplishment goals, you may consider the beneficial reasons for performing a task.

A wise strategy is to divide large jobs into smaller ones. A variation on this is to devote brief periods of time to a large work and complete as much as you can in that time with little anticipation of the results. For instance, try taking notes on ideas that spring to mind within a paper for approximately 10 minutes or skimming through a lengthy book to catch the key points alone. Once you've repeated this multiple times on a large assignment, you will have made some progress on it, gained momentum, and have less work to do to finish the task.

Be realistic. Changing your habits and achieving your objectives require time and work; avoid setting yourself up for failure by not being realistic in your expectations. If you're feeling stuck, you won't likely employ a schedule that serves as a constant reminder of all you need to get done and is all work and no play.

Create a flexible timetable that is primarily unstructured and only includes the things that are absolutely required. Record every minute you spend pursuing your objectives, and treat yourself as a reward. This can lessen feelings of overwhelm and boost satisfaction with the work you do.

Be aware of what you say and think to yourself.Talk to yourself in ways that help you stay focused on your objectives and that take the place of old, ineffective self-talk patterns. Say "I will..." rather than "I wish I hadn't."

Do you routinely put off doing the things you should? Your routines and procedures (or lack thereof), your desire to avoid unpleasant feelings (such as worry and boredom), or your own defective thought processes are likely the root causes of the issue (which can make a task seem harder than it is). Fortunately, there are straightforward methods for handling each.

For instance, complete your vital job in a regular rhythm every day to create excellent habits: "I follow this up with my serious work." Create a process for beginning new activities (drawing from ones you've completed successfully); this will make it simpler to get things going. When a task causes you anxiety, start with the simplest element and work your way up. You may also encourage yourself to complete a tedious activity by promising yourself a reward. If your thinking is stuck, think about what would make a task difficult, then come up with its opposite.

We all lament the shortness of time, yet we also have far more time than we know what to do with. Either we don't do anything at all, we don't do anything that serves a purpose, or we don't do anything that we should be doing. We constantly bemoan how short our days are while acting as though there would never be an end to them.

Establish a procedure for beginning new work. What about tasks you're taking on for the first time that seem out of your comfort zone? If you have a well-established method for addressing new jobs, you'll be less likely to put them off. You'll develop your own particular form of habit when you face something new, which will lessen decision fatigue over where to begin.

In times of ambiguity, this reaction is intensified. When you're stressed out, you're more likely to put anything off. Even straightforward chores, like responding to emails, might feel difficult in this mood.

In order to determine whether your emotions are the main cause of your procrastination, ask yourself, "How am I feeling mentally?" Do the tasks I avoid elicit any particular feelings? Do they bore, enrage, frighten, or make me feel resentful? Untangle your emotions. You can better control your emotions if you can accurately recognise them, a concept known as "emotional granularity" by psychologists. Analyzing the degree to which each emotion is influencing your attitude toward a task is helpful when it comes to procrastination.

If you struggle in certain areas but are generally disciplined in others, certain thought patterns may be to blame. For example, many people tend to underestimate the intricacy of activities that have extended deadlines. However, certain cognitive characteristics that contribute to procrastination are quite personal. One of my personal troublesome patterns is as follows: I have a tendency to assume that my other work is bad when someone praises a particular piece of it, which makes me anxious when it's time to write again—even though I've just gotten praise! Asking yourself this question can help you determine whether cognitive blockages are a factor in your procrastination. Does the task feel more difficult than the steps really are, given my abilities?

My personal system follows the same stages consistently: I start by thinking about three possible approaches to the issue. I then perform a premortem analysis to determine what is most likely to go wrong. I then determine how much time I should allot to the work. Finally, I look for quick methods to test my hypotheses.

Reverse brainstorming has evolved into one of my favourite strategies, despite the fact that I didn't use it much until I included it in my book, Stress-Free Productivity.

When used in relation to procrastination, it is imagining how you would make your work impossible to do or how you would truly want to avoid completing it. You may then come up with their opposites, which will help you feel less blocked after you have the solutions.

For instance, if I picture having to complete a task flawlessly the first time or in the same manner as a colleague I respect, it can seem impossible. On the other hand, recognising that mistakes and flaws will occur and going about it my way, utilising my unique skills, will make the work appear simpler.

Consider all the ways that the work you're putting off is comparable to one you can complete simply and successfully as another fast reframing strategy. For instance, I'm totally at ease writing blog entries but not presentations.

The ability to start is the only trait that comes to mind as being more essential to the active pursuit of a healthy life. Strong relationships, bright creativity, important employment, a physically active lifestyle, and everything else that denotes a happy, healthy, and satisfied life all require the ability to start over again. Be aware that playing the game is more important than becoming the greatest if you want to be happy or content.

However, both involve conveying a few points quickly, speaking in a casual manner, sharing tales, and inspiring the audience to identify with you. Here, it's important to specify the analogies precisely, as I have done.

Accept hard effort and accept friction. Tasks that are simple, familiar, and relatively productive may feel more rewarding than tasks that are novel, more difficult, but have greater potential value. Because of this, we frequently decide to do unimportant tasks rather than taking on tasks that would have a greater impact.

Avoid the error of confusing productivity with labour that is free of friction. For instance, diverse teams frequently come up with greater ideas but may also face more conflict. Friction is a common feature of novel labour, which by its very nature delays progress and can be stressful. This results in an emotional reasoning mistake, which occurs when you extrapolate too much from your emotions. For example, you can think you're going the wrong way or not making enough progress when you feel anxious and challenged. Understanding this phenomenon and how to spot it when it affects you are crucial. You may avoid making mistakes in thinking by being conscious of your own thought processes, or "metacognition."

Remember that even though it may not seem like it, if you show up to perform a critical job and approach it as strategically as you can, you will make progress. You'll procrastinate less if you can tolerate difficult work better. Make a commitment to working on the task with the most potential each day, even if it causes erratic emotions and thoughts.

Naturally, delaying anything indicates that you are doing something against your better judgment. Tell me, if this was something you truly wanted to accomplish, would you put it off or postpone it? Of course, you'd preempt it!

Have you ever observed that if someone is waiting for someone they really want to meet, they will check their watch 25 times in the first 10 minutes alone? Why? due to their desire to postpone it. You are doing something you don't want to be doing, so you want to put things off.

Why are you engaging in a behaviour that you find objectionable? Let me tell you that there is truly nothing to achieve in this life if you are simply doing it because you believe you will gain anything from it. You either lived this life wholeheartedly or you didn't. What will you ultimately receive?

Depending on the culture you came from, they will either bury you, burn you, or give you to the animals. Or do you believe you'll receive a reward at the conclusion? In the end, nothing will take place. What matters is how well you handled your life's journey. You must thus identify what it is that you truly want to achieve. If you discover that one item, you will never put anything off and never postpone anything.

According to a piece on "Psychology Today," we have all experienced wanting to do a task but delaying it until a later date. Sometimes we put off starting a project because we just don't care enough about it, while other times we care a great deal yet nevertheless choose to work on something else.

Everyone delays work occasionally, but many individuals purposefully seek out distractions—which, regrettably, are more readily available—in order to avoid undertaking challenging chores. Procrastination is mostly a reflection of our ongoing fight with self-control and our inability to foresee our feelings for the upcoming day or tomorrow.

Some people compliment my work ethic, but others claim I put in excessive hours and like my job. Naturally, this trait of mine has given me both friends and foes. I don't like slackers. I hate lazy individuals; dislike isn't the appropriate word.

Naturally, there are moments when we feel lethargic and are just not in the mood for work, but when this behaviour develops into a habit, it becomes something altogether different. You already know I work hard, so you should also be aware of my propensity for putting things off. I put things off a lot.

By recognising and comprehending the feelings you experience when confronted with a job or scenario that forces you to go outside of your comfort zone, you may overcome procrastination. You have the ability to silence the voice of doom and gloom that undermines your efforts to complete the necessary tasks.

Even though I don't like to admit it (speaking things into existence and all), I do go above and beyond the average procrastinator. There are several effective methods for overcoming procrastination. Trick yourself by giving yourself an extra 10 minutes to complete the work. Make a vision board and use apps, screen savers, and "to do" lists to remind yourself.

The lag between intention and execution is known as procrastination. To beat procrastination and get the happiness you genuinely deserve, you can decide to take action. If you follow your joy, the universe will open doors for you where there were only walls.

Protect yourself by dividing the work into manageable bits rather than letting yourself become overwhelmed by its immensity. Imagine that you have already accomplished your objective. Then, step into it and enjoy the satisfaction.

Keep your vow to improve yourself and strive to be your best self. Are the things you are doing today helping you get closer to your goals? The next time you feel self-doubt, stop yourself and feel it! Take it on! Stop listening to those who are always negative. Use positive affirmations Now, nothing can stop me. "It's up to me if it's to be!"

I've listened to motivational speeches, read a lot of books and articles about how to break this habit, and watched a number of Ted Talks on the subject of procrastination on YouTube.

To achieve anything in this world worth doing, we must jump in and climb through as best we can, rather than standing back trembling and thinking about the cold and danger.

According to Valerie Brown, TedTalks speaker, "we live in a world where everyone wants everything right away, and procrastinators are not among those who value immediate gratification." She gives us examples of famous procrastinators such as Leonardo Da Vinci, who spent 16 years creating the Mona Lisa and once considered himself a failure. She offers us an alternative viewpoint on procrastinators, arguing that it isn't always detrimental to one's job or health.

The accidental procrastinators and the purposeful procrastinators are two classifications of procrastinators. We can place Thomas Edison in the latter group and Leonardo da Vinci in the former. We can refer to those who postpone as having a supersonic jigsaw puzzle unlocked in their heads; this indicates that when someone procrastinates and keeps thinking about it, thousands of thoughts enter their heads. You may label Aristotle and Salvador Dali as purposeful procrastinators who put off tasks in order to produce more creative work.

One of the greatest thieves of joy is the habit of continually delaying an experience until you can afford it, until the moment is perfect, or until you know how to accomplish it.

I would offers humorous perspective on procrastination and delves deeply into the mentality of a procrastinator. Adam Grant, another popular key note speaker in tedtalks, continued by explaining to the audience that whereas "precrastinators" have a logical decision-maker, "procrastinators" have two more beings in their heads: the "immediate gratification monkey" and "the panic monster."

Adam Grant strikes a balance between "precrastinators" and "procrastinators" in his talk, expanding on the ideas of the "immediate gratification monkey" and "the panic monster" and giving life to a productive and creative character. He uses Martin Luther King Jr.'s postponement of drafting his speech as an illustration of how many notable people throughout history were procrastinators. The leader's original words, "I have a dream," were not part of the script; by deviating from the plan, he left himself up to all possibilities. When you go further into the relationship between original thinkers and procrastinators, you may understand how one must be better and different than the other to advance something forward.

A poll found that 20% of Americans are habitual procrastinators. Contrary to popular opinion, research after research demonstrates that persistent procrastination is a result of unpleasant feelings such as guilt, anxiety, sadness, and low self-worth and not only of laziness and bad time management.

"Procrastination is the killer of opportunities." -Victor K. Kiam

Do You Put Things Off? Almost everyone has occasionally failed to carry out their pledges or goals. We all favour benefits today over those in the future and give the future a lower priority than it deserves. Or, to put it another way, we frequently behave against our own interests. Let's examine how to use Enkrateia and defeat Akrasia.

Reduce your habit size to avoid creating difficulties. Build a ritual with all of your heart and soul, and make it as simple as you can to begin. Wait until you've perfected the skill of showing up before you worry about the outcomes. Focus on your timetable rather than your scope to accomplish this. Our brains favour short-term rewards above long-term gains. In your own life, for instance, if you want to read one chapter every day but are unable to allot enough time to finish one whole chapter, aim to read for at least 15 minutes. Instead of scoping your aim, time-slot it.

"Postponement often involves greater risk than making the wrong choice."- Theodore A. Hopf

Create small milestones to increase momentum for the following reasons:

1. You are more likely to complete big undertakings since small steps forward help to retain momentum over time.
2. The more rapidly you finish a task that is productive, the more quickly your day takes on a productive and successful mindset.

Using commitment gadgets, plan your future course of action. Commitment gadgets can help you plan your future activities. Instead of depending on willpower in the heat of the moment, look for ways to automate your behaviour in advance. Rather than becoming a victim of your future behaviours, take control of them. A personal example: You can routinely invest through a systematic investing plan

(SIP) by setting up an automated transfer of cash to your investment account. An example from the world of work is the early warning system. Predictive analytics, risk management, metrics, and dependency setting while scheduling are some of the instruments in our professional toolbox that will allow us to fulfil our obligations.

To put it simply, create a chain of daily progress on your most essential task and have it posted such that it will stimulate you rather than cause you to slack off. Choose a new routine and mark an X on the calendar for each day you follow it. This strategy aims to support your constancy and prolong your string of excellent deeds. In the workplace, visual dashboards and process flow diagrams may help you understand where you are and where the bottlenecks are.

In order to increase and maintain long-term productivity, create time assets rather than time debts. The majority of productivity solutions emphasise immediate effectiveness. However, we must create time assets rather than time debts if we want to increase productivity over the long run. The decisions or activities you take now that will save you time later are known as "time assets."

You have a method for managing your time thanks to Time Assets and Time Debts. Time assets are a fantastic illustration of why systems are more crucial than objectives. Every asset you create is a system that works continuously for you. You can work as hard as you want, but it won't matter if your calendar is full of time debt. Your decisions will keep you from being productive.

But if you deliberately accumulate time assets every day, your time will expand rapidly. In the workplace, automation is a prime illustration of a time asset. You just need to build a programme, utility, or script once today, and it will perform processes for you repeatedly each day after that. A time commitment is made up front, and daily rewards are received after that. Automating bill payments and setting up standing orders will reduce the amount of work required to pay the bills. The decisions or activities you do now that will take up more time later on are called "time debts." Both in one's personal and professional life: The majority of individuals spend time each day sending and receiving emails. Sending an email now implies that you'll read the response and maybe react again at a later time. Every email you send incurs a little debt that you must settle in the future.

Planning for failure doesn't imply you anticipate failing; rather, it means you have a plan in place for what you'll do and how you'll get back on track if things don't go as planned. You're in an all-or-nothing trap if your attention is on being flawless. The If-Then Technique is the ideal technique to prepare for disappointment and stay committed to your objectives even when things get wild. Why? Because you really need to do so, it compels you to develop a plan for lowering the scope while maintaining the timetable. It's a good method to make yourself intentional about your practise rather than just putting in the time. If I don't get up in time to run tomorrow morning, I'll run after work. If I purchase a bad lunch, I'll prepare a good supper. If risk X occurs, I will put in place Y a mitigation strategy and Z a contingency plan. These two opposing viewpoints constitute the paradox: If I start early, the project will consume all of the time I allot until the deadline date. I'll probably spend longer on it than necessary as a result. If I wait and give myself less time, I might say that I didn't give myself enough time if the project is a failure.

Divide big undertakings into manageable, modest jobs. You've heard the joke about how to devour an elephant. at a time, one mouthful. You'll feel empowered and motivated to keep going if you succeed in completing tiny portions of the bigger endeavor. Small activities allow you to build on accomplishments and lessen the sensation of overwhelm that comes with a difficult endeavour.

Consider what needs to be done each evening. Estimate the time it will take to perform each job on your list. Make sure to estimate highly. Usually, things take a bit longer than we anticipate. We appear to spend more time than we intended due to interruptions, distractions, and technological glitches. Give each item on your list a level of difficulty. You may make up your own scale, or you can just use the numbers 1 through 3 to indicate difficulty.

Establish specified timeframes to do your task. Put meetings and other definite commitments on your calendar. Next, give the tasks on your to-do list a priority. You may complete things more quickly by scheduling specified work times on your calendar. Additionally, you'll discover that planning your day helps you understand that there is plenty of time to engage in activities you like (reading, dinner with the family, watching a movie, etc.). Your calendar is a useful tool that will act as your daily guide.

Take into account the times of day that you are most awake and focused. Everyone has times when they perform at their best. Simply put, it's the time of day when you can concentrate the best and do your most difficult tasks. Plan your most difficult chores during these times, but make sure to schedule regular pauses. Plan simpler tasks to be completed in the late afternoon if you start to feel drained and sluggish.

Francesco Cirillo developed this time-management technique in Italy in the 1980s. According to the method, you should set a timer for 25 minutes of focus and then 5 minutes of relaxation. If 25 to 20 minutes is your ideal working time, you may use this as a reference or change it. According to more recent studies, the ideal combination is 52 minutes of intensive effort followed by 17 minutes of relaxation.

Next time, take the time to plan rather than attempting to handle everything at once or diving immediately into a massive job. By breaking up larger jobs into smaller ones, you'll be able to achieve a number of little accomplishments that you can build on. Additionally, it considerably lessens the tension that increases when we believe we are out of time or condemned to failure. Since taking the first step is typically the most difficult, start small.

Procrastination is addressed by psychology in a number of ways. Procrastination and personality characteristics are related. Conscientiousness is one of the Big Five traits, and those who score highly in it are less likely to procrastinate because they score higher in traits like self-control, diligence, a sense of duty, tenacity, and effective time management. People with a high level of integrity make good employees. Being a dispositional procrastinator is insufficient. The nature of the assignment must also be considered. Temporal discounting is the idea that activities that are far off in the future are given less weight in our priorities than chores that are right in front of us right now.

Assume you are standing in front of a large red button that, when pressed after t timesteps, will reward you with t units of usefulness. When should you push it if you want to get the most utility out of it? It is obvious that the answer is never, since touching it at any point would be less useful than waiting for another timestep. But obviously not never, as you would never receive any utility at all! An illustration of the procrastination paradox is this: These challenges are the kind of specification issues that arise when you require a system to do two incompatible tasks, such as pressing a button once and doing it later than at any other moment (aka never). These kinds of scenarios are crucial decision-theoretic conundrums that show how certain naive anticipated utility maximisers can utterly fail. They show that there isn't always an ideal normative choice process, which poses a problem for the comprehension and application of mechanical rationality. In fact, this essay sees the presence of such functions as a defence of utility functions generally.

Because of the misunderstanding that surrounds them, this essay seeks to establish a rigorous, original framework for comprehending and, ultimately, making serious peace with them. The good, the bad, and the ugly of these paradoxes are explored in this post after a thorough study of them in the context of decision theory and reinforcement learning formalisms.

An agent may be susceptible to procrastination paradoxes if it attempts to maximise an anticipated utility function that lacks a specified maximum that can be reached in a finite number of steps. Unfortunately, it may be quite easy to develop functions of supposed usefulness like this. For any decision-making process, creating a decision-making process that avoids procrastination traps is simple. The best method for handling procrastination problems does not exist. For procrastination situations where the limit of the achievable benefit is likewise infinite, some probabilistic solutions can prevent postponing indefinitely while still having infinite anticipated utility.

The majority of offered remedies miss the mark when it comes to procrastinators' methods of operation and try to modify them more quickly than their ingrained personality features would allow. However, structured procrastination is beneficial to the procrastinator. It's a paradoxical word that refers to the kind of procrastination that boosts your productivity by converting it from a weakness to a strength and may serve as a sort of "nuclear option" when all other productivity tips fail.

You ought to be completing that one "very important task," as the saying goes. The one that elicits recognisable resistance: "Please don't do this critical task! "Put off the task—this is the counterintuitive action to take. Give in to your tendency to put off something. Think about your to-do list in the interim. You should eventually complete a variety of tasks, all of varying importance. Put off the task—this is the counterintuitive action to take. Give in to your tendency to put off something.

Now that you've succumbed to the impulse to put something off, start working on a different item from your list that requires attention rather than engaging in glitzy time-wasters. The genius of the planned procrastination strategy is that it embraces rather than fights the enormous difficulty of altering the pro-tomorrow attitude.

You can use the desire to do anything other than the task at hand, which normally prompts you to organise your sock drawer or binge-watch Netflix, to drive productivity. With this kind of proper work structure, the procrastinator becomes a productive citizen and "a competent human being," according to Stanford philosophy professor John Perry, who authored a fantastic article about organised procrastination.

Working on the very important task first might be helpful for some people. But keep in mind that you are still engaging in the procrastinator's game, in which placing something first saps motivation to begin working on it. Therefore, the mental ruse is to prioritise other chores above the Very Important Task in order to make the decision simpler.

Instead, place tasks like arranging your workspace or mastering a new skill that appear highly important but have more forgiving deadlines at the top. Additionally, you'll probably discover that fresh very important tasks have been added to your list, making the original one appear even more appealing. The motivation to begin working on anything is sapped when it is prioritised at the top. Structured procrastination necessitates a significant amount of self-deception. In a sense, you are deceiving yourself into working while engaging in doublethink on the importance of a variety of tasks.

It turns out that procrastinators are frequently excellent self-deceivers, so that is not an issue. We get into problems because of our innate ability to manipulate our thoughts, which leads us to confuse our short-term and long-term objectives. The upside to all of this is that the terrible shame that often saps your motivation is instead turned into a source of energy. You'll notice that the procrastinator at heart has transformed into one of those very productive people as more things start getting done!

Procrastination is harmful, as everyone is aware. But being flawless is okay, right? Wrong. Both are challenging and frequently coexist, creating an endless cycle that may devastate both your productivity and your mental health.

Don't wait for ideal circumstances before beginning. Have faith that you have all the resources you need to start the project and that, once you get it underway, you'll find whatever extra resources you require. By "satisficing," you acknowledge that it will never be perfect. When you satisfy, your goal is to get outcomes that are only adequate and nothing more. This is particularly helpful if you, your group, or your business suffer from the mindset that "everything has to be flawless before we launch." Remember that you must begin somewhere. Your enterprise shares the same humble origins as many other spectacularly profitable endeavors. Remember the Make. Do. instruction. Don't wait until it's perfect before releasing your invention; you can always make changes afterwards. It could be too late by then.

Apply design thinking ideas to your need for perfection to geek out. The process is just as crucial in design thinking as the final output. Focus instead on the five design thinking steps: discovery, interpretation, ideation, iteration, and evaluation. Focus instead on the five design thinking steps: discovery, interpretation, ideation, experimentation/testing, and evolution/iteration. This will help you overcome your fear of "failure" surrounding the conclusion.

Making any or all of the aforementioned changes will start to assist you in overcoming perfectionistic inclinations, but the following recommendations will more directly attack the root causes of procrastination. You may need to conduct some research to identify the root of your unwillingness to complete the assignment. Take into consideration two helpful exercises:

Draw a line along the centre of a piece of paper. List the chores you are putting off and being blocked on in the first column. List any doubts, anxieties, or fears you have about completing the work in the second column. Write down as much as you can, starting anywhere you like.

Another way to do this is to make a list of the tasks, the actions necessary to complete each activity, and the issues you expect to face. Eliminating the unneeded can help reduce the overpowering emotions and ideas that cause procrastination. Distractions should be removed from the area, and everything that doesn't further your objectives should be delegated, dropped, or deleted. Shut yourself away. Gather only what you require to complete the assignment, leave your usual workspace, and head to a conference room, another office, the library, a co-working space, a friend's house, or any other location where you won't be interrupted by familiar faces and routines. Use a fantastic browser extension or tool to prevent yourself from being drawn to distracting websites. To avoid receiving any alerts, turn off your phone's ringtone or put it in aeroplane mode.

People often avoid doing new things because they want to do them well the first time. Despite being entirely unreasonable, unworkable, and impractical, this is the way that the majority of people spend their lives. It is known as the perfection syndrome.

According to Dr. McDowell, disrupting all-or-nothing thinking is necessary to combat perfectionism. For instance, if you're attempting to arrange your email, it won't help if you treat it as a single job. Determine the task's components, then break it down into manageable pieces. Making activities more doable by breaking them down into smaller components also increases the frequency with which you feel accomplished as you tick each item off your list. Consider it this way: You must organise your wedding.

For instance, you could be tempted to include "get flowers" as a chore, but doing so might make you feel overburdened. Sometimes the simple act of checking things off a list inspires us to work more. No job is too small for your list because of this! Searching for local florists on Google might be all it takes. Once it is crossed off, celebrate your success and continue to think positively. Small wins give you momentum! Therefore, organise your duties properly.

It's crucial to keep in mind that we frequently underestimate the amount of time it will take us to finish a task when it's towering over us and we've made it out to be a giant. You also have a tendency to forget to arrange time for self-care when you estimate that an activity that causes anxiety will take the entire day. According to registered clinical psychologist Dr. Supriya Blair, balancing priorities is crucial. "Due to this, we build time for social and self-care activities into our daily and weekly schedules." Due to this, we build time for social and self-care activities into our daily and weekly schedules. It requires experience, tolerance, and self-compassion to hold oneself accountable to complete jobs and enjoyable activities.

Numbers have power! Anything may be daunting, but doing it alone is worse than doing it with assistance. Whether it's your partner, a friend, a parent, or a child, working together with a supportive, dedicated partner is one of the greatest methods to get organised when you're feeling anxious.To gain some much-needed perspective, you can also get in touch with a therapist or life coach. You're not by yourself. According to Briana Mary Ann Hollis, LSW, the owner and director of Learning to Be Free, there are individuals out there who can assist. "Write down the task you now need assistance with, and then list at least one person who can assist you," she advises. This will demonstrate that you are not required to do all tasks on your own.

Although it's difficult for one person to devote themselves to everything, we frequently feel the need to win over everyone. A certain way to get overwhelmed and subsequently enter the same self-destructive cycle is to take on too many obligations. According to Angela Ficken, a psychologist who specialises in anxiety and OCD, "Think about where you might simplify your calendar, delegate to others, or even say no to activities and chores that are not imminent or essential." The purpose is to set certain restrictions on your schedule. By doing this, you may free up your time and thoughts so that you can engage in things that make you happy. "It is perfectly acceptable to say no," she continues. Everyone is busy and has commitments, so don't feel bad about declining an invitation to work on a project or get together with a college friend you haven't spoken to in 14 years.

You can always treat yourself, and doing so is frequently onc of the besl ways to motivate yourself to do organising tasks.

Dr. Nancy Irwin, a psychologist with Seasons in Malibu, advises her patients to "concentrate on how you will feel when your home is tidy and clean, how exciting and enjoyable it may be to plan your wedding, and how responsible you will feel when you do your taxes." How do you determine your limitations? If it's not a "hell yes," then it's a no. Is that a saying you've heard before? This is a useful guide to use while taking on duties; however, there are always exceptions to any norm. "Then treat yourself to a reward for a job well done." Positive reinforcement makes sure that the following project will go just as well and tells you that you are stronger than your nervousness.

I prepare a list of the assignments and housework I want to get done each day. They range from the simple, like "taking out the garbage," to the significant, like "finish editing" or "submit invoicing."

It may be quite helpful to be in sync with your body and attitude while you practise breaking habits. Self-check-ins are essential, especially if you have a tendency to focus on the minute details. It's crucial to take a step back and give yourself pauses and reminders to prevent feeling overburdened. For Ficken, mindfulness is essential. "Going for a stroll or sitting on your doorstep is a reasonably simple mindfulness technique." Being outside might serve as a simple visual and tactile signal to help you focus on the present. Keeping your feet on the ground is crucial for controlling your anxiety. When you feel your anxiety rising, don't be reluctant to take a break since both your body and brain need it. What should I keep in mind above all else? It's not just you.

In fact, anxiety disorders, which affect 40 million individuals annually, are the most prevalent mental ailment in the United States. You shouldn't feel alone if your anxiety is making it difficult for you to manage daily duties or organise your life. Millions of people worldwide experience the same problems. The good news is that tendencies that keep you stuck in a negative cycle may be broken and that anxiety disorders are often curable. Making the decision to be patient with yourself is the first step.

Despite the apparent significance of self-control, we shouldn't restrict our meaning of these phrases to only the strict management of the person's desires and cravings. As this can be an alternative to insanity, these phrases also refer to common sense, sober insight, restraint, and soundness of mind.

References

- *Procrastination Equation PB: How to Stop Putting Things Off and Start Getting Stuff Done Paperback – Illustrated, 3 January 2012 by Piers Steel PhD (Author).*
- *Time Management: Proven Strategies to Boost Productivity and Take Control of Your Time (The Best Life Handbook: A Self-Help Series for Building a Fulfilling Life) Kindle Edition by Dan Williams (Author).*
- *Rewire Your Brain: 2 Books in 1: Master Your Mindset For Success & Habit Hack Your Way To Happiness Paperback – Import, 20 January 2021 by Leon Lyons (Author).*
- *The Subtle Art of Not Giving a F*ck: A Counterintuitive Approach to Living a Good Life Paperback – 19 January 2017 by Mark Manson (Author).*
- *The Little Book on Time Management: Your Last Quick Read to Finally Beat Procrastination Once and for All Kindle Edition by John Cunloy (Author).*
- *How to Be Disciplined: The Beginner's Guide to Discovering How to Manage Time, Become More Productive, Overcome Procrastination, and Focus on the Things That Matter Most in Life Kindle Edition by Sheldon Howe (Author).*
- *Dopamine Detox : A Short Guide to Remove Distractions and Get Your Brain to Do Hard Things (Productivity Series Book 1) Kindle Edition by thibaut meurisse (Author), Kerry J Donovan (Editor), July 2021.*
- *The One Thing: The Suprisingly Simple Truth Behind Extraordinary Results Hardcover – 4 July 2013 by Gary Keller (Author), Jay Papasan (Author).*
- *How To Conquer Procrastination Paperback – Import, 27*

February 2013 by Dennis Harting (Author).

- *Do Hard Things: Why We Get Resilience Wrong and the Surprising Science of Real Toughness by Steve Magness (Author), June 2021.*
- *21 Keys To Develop A Productivity Plan & A Productive Mindset: A Guide To Overcome Your Bad Habits And Improve Your Time Management: Guide To Overcome ... how to increase your productivity Book 2) Kindle Edition by Rob Willis.*
- *The Time Management Solution: 21 Proven Tactics To Increase Your Productivity, Reduce Your Stress, And Improve Your Work-Life Balance! Kindle Edition by Damon Zahariades.*
- *Effects Of Cognitive Task Load On Prospective Judgment For Time Perception Paperback – Import, 2 September 2022 by Yadav Vishal (Author).*
- *Time Management: Discover Powerful Strategies to Increase Productivity, Master Your Habits, Amplify Focus, Beat Procrastination, and Eliminate Laziness for Achieving Your Goals!: 2 (Self Help Mastery) Paperback – Import, 1 March 2022 by Steve Martin.*
- *Productivity : Maximise Your Productivity, Increase Your Productivity and Achieve Success (100 Ways to Improve Your Productivity and Stop Procrastination) Kindle Edition by Mike C. Adams (Author).*
- *Productivity: Boost Productivity, Overcome Procrastination and Increase Time Management Kindle Edition by Nick Pierce (Author).*
- *Your Daily 7-Minute Focus: Increase Your Concentration and Productivity with Easy Habits (Personal Improvement, Book 1) Kindle Edition by William Rhein (Author).*
- *Time Management: 50 Proven Strategies To End Procrastination, Get Organized And Increase Your*

Productivity (Time Management Skills, Getting Things Done, ... Organization, Successful People Book 1) Kindle Edition by Rick Riley.

- *Procrastination Addiction: Time Management Strategies: Use Positive Psychology of Willpower Instinct. Increase Your Productivity, Organize Your Life and Change Your Habits.Stop Procrastinating Now! Kindle Edition by Alex Bradford (Author).*
- *Make your time right Paperback – 22 December 2020 by Kam Jgup (Author).*
- *Productivity: Overcome Laziness, Defeat Procrastination and Find Freedom From Stress (Learn How To Increase Your Productivity Even If Your Are Lazy) Kindle Edition by Harry Dsouza (Author).*
- *Stop Procrastination: Simple Habits to Increase Productivity and Get Things Done: 1 (How to Stop Procrastination and Laziness) Paperback – Import, 6 August 2019 by Megan Georgiana.*
- *Mind Management, Not Time Management: Productivity When Creativity Matters: 2 (Getting Art Done) Hardcover – Import, 19 November 2021 by David Kadavy (Author).*
- *How To Stop Procrastinating: Simple and effective methods to get over any task easily and on time Kindle Edition by William Richards (Author).*
- *Time Management - How to Multitask, Increase Productivity and Stop Procrastination : time management and organizational skills for men, women, students Kindle Edition by Lance MacNeil (Author).*
- *Procrastination: Ends now - 12 Secrets to Boost your Productivity, Increase Motivation and Develop New Habits in 21 Days Kindle Edition by Michael Zenstar (Author).*
- *Supercharge Productivity Habits: 50+ Simple Hacks to Organize Your Tasks, Overcome Procrastination, Increase*

Efficiency and Work Smarter to Become a Top Performer Hardcover – 25 June 2020 by John R Torrance (Author).

- *Unlocked Productivity: Learn How You Can Increase Productivity, Avoid Procrastination, Have More Free Time, Work Less And Make More Money (Unlocking Book 2) Kindle Edition by Andy R. Schwartz (Author).*
- *Stop Procrastination & Increase Productivity: 60 Tricks on How to Improve Your Focus, Time Management, Habits, Productivity and Overall Ability to Get ... a Time (Self-Help and Improvement Book 3) Kindle Edition by A.V. Mendez.*
- *Stop Procrastinating: Simple Steps to Increase Productivity and Overcome Procrastination (Time Management and Productivity Series) Kindle Edition by Robert Hensley (Author).*
- *The Procrastination Solution: 92 Great Ways to Overcome Procrastination, Manage Your Time, and Increase Productivity Kindle Edition by Max Goldwall (Author).*
- *Productivity Habits: Proven Techniques to Increase Personal Productivity and Achieve Goals (Time Management and Productivity Series) Kindle Edition by Robert Hensley (Author).*
- *Following Through: A Revolutionary New Model for Finishing Whatever You Start Paperback – February 1, 2015 by Steve Levinson Ph.D. (Author), Pete Greider M.Ed. (Author).*
- *Your Focus Formula: How to Successfully Stay on Task, Finish Projects and Achieve Your Goals Kindle Edition by Diana Fitts (Author).*
- *How to Set Goals with Kaizen & Ikigai: Focus, Cure Procrastination, & Increase Personal Productivity. Kindle Edition by Anthony Raymond.*
- *One Thing Paperback – International Edition, January 1, 2001 by Gary Keller (Author).*

- *The Willpower Instinct: How Self-Control Works, Why It Matters, and What You Can Do to Get More of It Paperback – Illustrated, December 31, 2013 by Kelly McGonigal (Author).*
- *Solving the Procrastination Puzzle: A Concise Guide to Strategies for Change Paperback – Illustrated, December 26, 2013 by Timothy A. Pychyl (Author).*
- *The Power of Habit: Why We Do What We Do in Life and Business Paperback – January 7, 2014 by Charles Duhigg (Author).*
- *The Productivity Project: Accomplishing More by Managing Your Time, Attention, and Energy Paperback – August 29, 2017 by Chris Bailey.*
- *Procrastination NO MORE!: Why Do You Procrastinate? Learn 27 Effective Strategies to Stop Procrastination, Increase Productivity and Get Things Done in Less Time: 3 (Personal Productivity) Paperback – Import, 16 August 2017 by Som Bathla (Author).*
- *Time Management: Proven Strategies To End Procrastination, Get Organized And Increase Your Productivity (Improve Your Time Management Skills) Paperback – Import, 30 July 2022 by Ronald Smith (Author).*
- *Productivity: Effective Ways To Overcome Procrastination And Improve Productivity In Order To Achieve Maximum Success (Reach Your Goals Without Procrastination) Paperback – Import, 3 December 2022 by Rayan Samper (Author).*
- *HOW TO BE PRODUCTIVE & OVERCOME PROCRASTINATION Paperback – 7 October 2021 by Arvind Upadhyay (Author).*
- *Time Management: Smart Hacks To Get Things Done, Stop Procrastination Habit And Increase Focus And*

Productivity: 1 (Productivity for Beginners) Paperback – 19 September 2018 by David Tracy (Author), Brian Allen (Author).

- *Why Has Nobody Told Me This Before?: The No 1 Sunday Times bestseller Paperback – Import, 6 January 2022 by Dr Julie Smith (Author).*
- *The procrastination cure code, Kindle Edition by Melissa Zack (Author) Format: Kindle Edition.*
- *HOW TO OVERCOME PROCRASTINATION: 10 Practical and Simple Ways of Effectively Managing Your Time and Eliminating Procrastination Forever. Kindle Edition by MILLIE BURTON (Author).*
- *Daily Self-Discipline: Stop Procrastination by Developing Habits and Building Daily Goals Paperback – Import, 14 February 2020 by Dorothy Mok (Author).*
- *Solving the Procrastination Puzzle: A Concise Guide to Strategies for Change Paperback – Illustrated, 26 December 2013 by Timothy A. Pychyl (Author).*
- *Do the Hard Things First: How to Win Over Procrastination and Master the Habit of Doing Difficult Work Paperback – Import, 15 June 2021 by Scott Allan (Author).*
- *The Now Habit: A Strategic Program for Overcoming Procrastination and Enjoying Guilt-Free Play Paperback – Illustrated, 5 April 2007 by Neil Fiore (Author).*
- *Stop Procrastinating: A Simple Guide to Hacking Laziness, Building Self Discipline, and Overcoming Procrastination Paperback – Import, 13 April 2018 by Nils Salzgeber (Author).*
- *The Art of Self-Discipline: Beat Procrastination, Break Bad Habits, and Achieve Your Goals Kindle Edition by Kimberly Olson (Author).*
- *TIME MANAGEMENT and The Art of overcoming*

Procrastination: A top of 10 Secrets on how to be more proactive, SMART and have clear and achievable goals Kindle Edition by Jordan J (Author).

- *The Art of Stopping Procrastination: Overcome Procrastination with Easy Strategies Paperback – Import, 25 August 2021 by Melanie Peppers (Author).*
- *The Anti-procrastination Habit Workbook: A Practical Guide to Mastering Your Time and Boosting Your Productivity (Procrastination Cure Book) Paperback – Import, 2 September 2017 by Vicky Norah (Author).*
- *Procrastination: What It Is, Why It's a Problem, and What You Can Do About It (APA LifeTools) Paperback – Import, 26 July 2022.*
- *Finish What You Started: Beat Procrastination, End Laziness, Get Things Done and Never Relapse Kindle Edition by Matt Rosen (Author) Format: Kindle Edition.*
- *End Procrastination Now!: Unleash the Self-Improved You Paperback – Import, 25 November 2014 by Emma Shaw (Author).*
- *The Science of Getting Started: How to Beat Procrastination, Summon Productivity, and Stop Self-Sabotage Paperback – Import, 7 December 2019 by Peter Hollins (Author).*
- *Procrastinator= Time's killer : Procrastination is committed when a procrastinator procrastinates. kindle edition by Reena J. Bisht (author) Format: kindle edition.*
- *Stop Procrastinating: An Easy-to-Follow Approach to Overcoming Procrastination, Building Self-Discipline, and Taking Action in Your Life (2022 Guide for Beginners) Paperback – 24 November 2022 by Grace Marshall (Author).*
- *by Fuschia M. Sirois (Author)Procrastination Cure Paperback – 8 October 2021 by Damon Goleman*

(Author).

- *Master Self-Discipline with 7 Powerful Exercises: Daily Blueprint to Cure Procrastination, Laziness, and Develop Atomic Habits to Achieve Goals for Entrepreneurs, Weight Loss, and Success in 10 Days Paperback – Import, 5 January 2020 by Stephen Mark (Author).*
- *Kill That Procrastination Habit: The Procrastination Remedy for Effective Time Management, Productivity boosting and Consciously Building Resourcefulness Kindle Edition by David Davidson (Author).*
- *Instantly Stop Procrastination: 4 Powerful Concepts That Will Help You Effectively Complete the Tasks You Keep Avoiding Kindle Edition by Patrick Drechsler (Author).*
- *The On-Time, On-Target Manager: How a "Last-Minute Manager" Conquered Procrastination Hardcover – 6 January 2004 by Ken Blanchard (Author), Steve Gottry (Author).*
- *The Power of Daily Self-Discipline and The No-Excuses Mindset: Practical Exercises to Strengthen Your Willpower and Overcome Procrastination by Creating Atomic Habits Hardcover – Import, 20 January 2020 by Ethan Grant (Author).*
- *The Freedom Manifesto. 28 November 2022 by Karan Bajaj (Author).*
- *Procrastination Be Gone: How to Count to Ten, Stop Procrastinating, and Become More Productive Kindle Edition by Chloe Evans (Author).*
- *Eat That Frog!: 21 Great Ways to Stop Procrastinating and Get More Done in Less Time [Paperback] Brian Tracy Paperback – 21 August 2018 by Brian Tracy (Author).*
- *The Procrastinatorâ€™s Mind Paperback – 1 February 2020 by Balivada (Author).*
- *Overcoming Procrastination Kindle Edition by Haruna D.*

Dahiru (Author).

- *Procrastination: Self Development Guide to Break the Procrastination Habit, Boost Productivity, Better Time Management and Use Psychology of Motivation to Cure Laziness and Get Things Done Paperback – Import, 3 June 2020 by Cal Tracy (Author).*
- *Do It Today: Overcome procrastination, improve productivity and achieve more meaningful things [Paperback] Foroux, Darius Paperback – 27 October 2020 by Darius Foroux (Author).*
- *STOP AKRASIA Paperback – 25 January 2022 by Joseph Neyyan (Author).*
- *How to Stop Procrastinating: A Proven Guide to Overcome Procrastination, Cure Laziness & Perfectionism, Using Simple 5-Minute Practices Paperback – Import, 4 August 2020 by Chase Hill (Author), Scott Sharp (Author).*
- *50 Things to Know to Stop Procrastination: Act Now & Procrastinate No More Kindle Edition by Kristine Joy Escarilla (Author), 50 Things To Know (Author).*
- *The End of Procrastination: How to Stop Postponing and Live a Fulfilled Life Paperback – 31 December 2018 by Petr Ludwig (Author), Adela Schicker (Author).*
- *Self-Discipline: Blueprint to Success in 10 Days for Entrepreneurs, Weight Loss and Overcome Procrastination, Laziness, Addiction: Achieve Any Goal with Powerful Long Term Daily Habits and Exercises Audible Logo Audible Audiobook – Unabridged Stephen Patterson (Author, Publisher), Russell Newton (Narrator).*
- *The Psychology of Procrastination: Understand Your Habits, Find Motivation, and Get Things Done Perfect Paperback – 1 January 2022 by Hayden Finch PhD (Author).*
- *Never Put it Off! : A Guide to Overcoming Procrastination*

and Achieving Success (The Path To Self-Empowerment) Kindle Edition by Kathyrn Blakemore (Author).

- *Procrastination: Breaking Free Paperback – 1 January 2013 by Leadstart Publishing Private Limited (Author).*
- *The Power of Daily Self-Discipline and The No-Excuses Mindset: Practical Exercises to Strengthen Your Willpower and Overcome Procrastination by Creating Atomic Habits Hardcover – Import, 20 January 2020 by Ethan Grant (Author).*
- *Kill Procrastination Forever: Simple Guided Method to Overcome Procrastination Paperback – 7 April 2022 by Growth Tracker (Author).*
- *Murder Procrastination Paperback – 6 September 2022 by Sanjay Kumar Agarwal (Author).*
- *Perfectionism Workbook: Proven Strategies to End Procrastination, Accept Yourself, and Achieve Your Goals Paperback – 24 July 2018 by Taylor Ma Newendorp (Author).*
- *The Procrastination Cure: : Simple Strategies for Overcoming Delay and Achieving Success Kindle Edition by Steve Remington (Author) Format: Kindle Edition.*
- *Procrastination Elimination: Seven Days to Action! Paperback – Import, 22 March 2005 by Susan Lynn Perry (Author).*
- *Cure for Procrastination Paperback – 28 December 2021 by Vijay Patidar (Author).*
- *Immediate Action: 7 Proven Hacks to Declutter Your Mind & Overcome Procrastination, Master Your Time & Get More Done in Less Paperback – 28 September 2022 by Ravi L Tewari (Author).*
- *Breaking The Procrastination Spell : Take a vow to do it NOW Paperback – 1 January 2021 by Arwa Rajgarhwala (Author).*

- *Procrastination The Opportunity Killer - A Self Assessment Guide And Workbook Paperback – 1 January 2013 by Amit Abraham (Author).*
- *How To Get From Where You Are To Where You Want To Be Paperback – 18 June 2007 by Jack Canfield (Author).*
- *From procrastination to productivity : The role of micro habits in achieving your goals Kindle Edition by Bright Clear (Author).*
- *Do It Now!: Break the Procrastination Habit Paperback – 8 January 1998 by William J. Knaus (Author).*
- *The Art of Self Discipline: Strategies for Overcoming Procrastination and Achieving Your Goals. Learn How to Build Your Mental Toughness Starting Today. Kindle Edition by Eric Williams (Author).*
- *17 Anti-Procrastination Hacks: How to Stop Being Lazy, Overcome Procrastination, and Finally Get Stuff Done Kindle Edition by Dominic Mann (Author).*
- *PROCRASTINATION: THE WAY OUT: Secrets to increasing time productivity Kindle Edition by Richmond Harry (Author).*
- *DO IT NOW!!!: The ultimate guide to help you overcome procrastination Kindle Edition by Dorothy D. Kimmel (Author).*
- *OVERCOMING PROCRASTINATION Paperback – 31 October 2021 by Windy Dryden (Author).*
- *Reboot : How to Manage Career Breaks and Return with Greater Success Paperback – 5 November 2022 by Issac John (Author).*
- *Soon: An Overdue History of Procrastination, from Leonardo and Darwin to You and Me Paperback – 31 March 2018 by Andrew Santella (Author).*
- *What Motivates Getting Things Done: Procrastination, Emotions, and Success Paperback – Import, 8 October*

2018 by Mary Lamia (Author).

- *How to Beat Procrastination in the Digital Age Paperback – Import, 25 November 2011 by Dr Linda Sapadin (Author).*
- *Immediate Action : A 7-Day Plan to Overcome Procrastination and Regain Your Motivation (Productivity Series Book 2) Kindle Edition by Thibaut Meurisse (Author).*
- *Self-Discipline in 60 Minutes: 7 Simple Habits for Overcoming Procrastination, Building Self-Control, and Achieving Goals Kindle Edition by William Jacobson (Author).*
- *How To Fall Asleep: Overcome Bedtime Procrastination, Stop Binge Watching and Social Media Scrolling When You Should Go To Bed... and Reclaim Your Life Kindle Edition by Matt Rosen (Author).*
- *How to conquer procrastination: Simplified solution to procrastination for students Kindle Edition by Losley Costa (Author).*
- *The Hard Thing About Hard Things: Building a Business When There Are No Easy Answers Kindle Edition by Ben Horowitz (Author), March 2014.*
- *Deep Work: Rules for focused success in a distracted world, paperback – 15 january 2016 by Cal Newport.*
- *How to Step Outside Your Comfort Zone: Stop procrastinating, become productive, get things done, and chase your goals (Lean Productivity Books) Kindle Edition by Maxim Dsouza, Sep 2021.*
- *Productivity Guide: The Only Path For You Is UP (productivity, productivity apps, ebooks, online books, buy ebooks, ebooks online, cheap books,) Kindle Edition by John Richlove (Author).*
- *How To Meet Your Deadlines: Be punctual, be disciplined,*

be time conscious and get things done as per schedule (Lean Productivity Books) Kindle Edition by Maxim Dsouza (Author).

- *The Power of Productivity: Maximize Productivity Through Adjusting Your Work Methods - For Students and Business People (productivity, business, extreme ... power, success, law of success) Kindle Edition by Samuel Atkins (Author).*
- *Procrastination Workbook: 20 Interactive Strategies to Stop Wasting Time, Build Self-Discipline and Overcome Procrastination Paperback – Import, 11 January 2021 by Walter D Marshall.*
- *Find Your Passion: Live the Way you Want and Discover Your Purpose (Productivity Books Book 1) Kindle Edition by Logan Hawkins (Author).*
- *Find Your Max: Improve Work Productivity with Time Management Magic (Productivity Books Book 2) Kindle Edition by Logan Hawkins (Author).*
- *Minimalist lifestyle: Minimalism 101, Declutter your Life, Ultimate Productivity Guide (Minimalism books, declutter, productivity,Minimal) Kindle Edition by Jennifer Gilbert (Author).*
- *Self-Discipline Mastery: Master Self-Discipline Like a Warrior and Gain Confidence, Motivation, and Happiness! (Self Discipline, Self Discipline Books, ... Productivity, Positive Psychology) Kindle Edition by Johnathon Anderson (Author).*
- *Writer's Guide to Procrastination: How to Conquer the Top 20 Excuses and Finally Write Your Book Today! Kindle Edition by Joseph Geran III (Author).*
- *Productivity Protocol And Eliminating Procrastination In The Process (Productivity, Productivity ... Management, Procrastination Cure, Success) Kindle Edition by Gary Johnson (Author).*

- *How to Stop Procrastinating: Powerful Strategies to Overcome Laziness and Multiply Your Time Paperback – Import, 29 October 2020 by Daniel Walter (Author).*
- *Checklist for Effective Mornings: Make Your Morning Productive And Get Things Done (Lean Productivity Books) Kindle Edition by Maxim Dsouza (Author).*
- *Time Management for the Organizationally Challenged: Increase Your Productivity 10X and Your Happiness 100X (Time management,time management books,productivity, procrastination,time management skills) Kindle Edition by Steve Graham (Author).*
- *Production: Simple Super Effective Tactics to Increase Productivity, Focus, Time Management & Cure Procrastination Fast (Productivity Hacks- Productivity ... Productivity Ninja- Productivity Books) Kindle Edition by Neo Monefa (Author).*
- *Productivity Books: Become Extremely Productive, Conquer Your Inner Procrastinator And Get More Done With These Practical Guides (Productivity Books, Procrastination Books, Time Management Books) Kindle Edition by Adam Richards (Author).*
- *Do the Work: Overcome Resistance and Get Out of Your Own Way Paperback – 10 March 2015 by Steven Pressfield (Author), Seth Godin (Foreword).*
- *Smarter Faster Better: The Secrets of Being Productive Kindle Edition by Charles Duhigg (Author).*
- *Productivity Hacks Unleashed - Brilliant Life Hacks To Increase Productivity, Improve Time Management, Save Money And Live A Better Life (Life Hacks, Productivity Hacks Book Kindle Edition by Alex Wild (Author).*
- *The crazy busy cure: a productivity book for people with no time for productivity books Paperback – 31 July 2021 by Zena Everett (Author).*

- *Productivity Superhero: Become the Most Organized and Disciplined Person You Know Paperback – 20 January 2019 by Dan Luca (Author).*
- *20 Ways To Create New Success Quickly: Tips on Happiness, Money, Productivity, and Learning (The New Success Series Book 1) Kindle Edition by Amier Aldelemy (Author).*
- *The productivity revolution: Control your time and get things done! Paperback – 20 September 2019 by Marc Reklau (Author).*
- *Empty The Bucket: Get things done and beat procrastination Kindle Edition by Nishkarsh Sharma (Author).*
- *Task Management Through the Eisenhower Matrix: A Task Management Notebook Paperback – Import, 14 July 2019 by Iliaca (Author).*
- *Understanding Human Behavior: The Complete Guide to Human Behavior, Personality Types, and Body Language Mastery Hardcover – Import, 10 August 2020 by Jason Miller (Author).*
- *How To Uplift Your Productivity In 7 Days: Improve your prioritization, time management skills and get things done (Lean Productivity Books) Kindle Edition by Maxim Dsouza (Author).*
- *The Productivity Project: Accomplishing More by Managing Your Time, Attention, and Energy Paperback – 29 August 2017 by Chris Bailey (Author).*
- *Extreme Productivity: Boost Your Results, Reduce Your Hours Paperback – 6 April 2021by Robert C. Pozen (Author).*
- *Prioritization: How to Prioritize Tasks to Increase Productivity and Work Smarter, Not Harder Paperback – 21 October 2014 by Geoffrey Wright (Author).*

About The Author

Dr. Amit Das, is a renowned executive advisor, consultant, educationist, author, speaker, counsellor, and coach whose 25+ years of business experience provides high-impact, practical solutions that support his clients' leadership development and organisational transformations. He worked for fortune 500 companies and left rich leagacy of organising transformational learning workshops. He has transformed more than 5000+ working executives through his path breaking capability building learning workshops. Dr. Amit Das is recognised as an innovative, principled thought leader who combines intellectual rigor and discipline with an ability to translate theory into practice. His operational skills are coupled with a strategic ability to analyse, develop, and implement successful strategies for profitability, growth, and sustainability.

Dr. Amit Das has a successful track record in aligning learning and training solutions to key business strategy with a strong focus on flawless execution excellence to facilitate individual, business divisional, and organisational performance. He keeps relentless focus on measuring training impact and ROI, people capability building graphs, training process governance, performance coaching, and strategic thinking. These have been some of his key individual success traits. His core capabilities include performance coaching, designing training and development frameworks, psychometric assessment and analysis, competency framework development and assessments, content design and facilitation of soft skills and leadership programmes, Learning Management Systems, Learning Impact Measurement, Talent Analysis, and Performance Coaching and Counselling.

Dr. Amit Das has authored multiple management and self-development books, like You Are Born To Succeed, Reinventing and Redefining You, Change Your Perspective Change Your Life, 90 Minutes Mindfulness, The Alchemy Of Resilient Leadership, Redefining Organisational Excellence, High Impact Leadership, A Divorce-Free Married Life, Redefining Corporate Spectrum, Create Your Leadership Edge, Love-Laugh- Live With Happiness, SMART Parenting @ Zero Cost, Redefining HRM, Building Organisational Capability, Ethical Road Map, Attomic Attention, BYPB, Redefining The Power Of Mentoring, Making The Most Future Fit Organisation, Redefining Talent Management, Defining Your Success Factors, Lead or Plead, Make The Most Of Your Life, Better Half or Bitter Half, Psychology Of Learning And Development, The Transformative Mind & Soul are few of them.

He has a Ph.D. and a Fellowship in strategic learning, along with his first class degrees in Human Resource Management, Marketing Management, International Business, and Corporate Laws from the top business schools in India. He is a certified Psychometric analyst, HR Analyst, OD Interventionist, Human Psychologist, Lifecoach, Leadership Developer, Black Belt (LSS), Strategic Thinker, Talent Analyst, certified professional trainer from the U.K. and certified behavioral coach from the U.S.A.

Dr. Amit Das teaches courses related to Organisational Development, Human Resource Management, Self-Management, and Leadership Coaching. He regularly engages in consulting and training work for organisation and leadership development with organisations across industries and with many institutions of higher education. He has published many research articles in the fields of human resource management, business compliance at the workplace, mindfulness, the business-society interface, and the best practises in management in reputed journals.

Dr. Amit Das likes googling, reading books, writing articles & books, cooking, listening to old melodies, and counselling people to unleash their true potential to build a strong nation. He is married and blessed with a son. He would love to hear about your experience after reading his books. You can email him and share your thoughts, or you can use his services for life coaching, positive behavioural counseling, educational support, and mentoring for young, promising students pursuing their B.B.A. and M.B.A. degrees.

His insightful, funny, and brutally honest writings about success and failure, self-awareness, and interpersonal relationships have established him as one of the top personal brands. He is an authorpreneur and content producer. The main concepts that have driven his journey—which started with him wanting to be an IIM professor and concluded with him producing material that has been viewed and read by millions—are collected in his book. His opinions cover a wide range of topics, including the value of forming habits for long-term success, the cornerstones of self-management, embracing and accepting failure, and the unvarnished truth about developing empathy. This is a book that you should read and reread, highlight, and ponder over and over again. You should also gift this book to your family, friends, and random strangers. He wants this book to go down in history as the most talented one ever!

9 798889 518716